Clear**Revise**®

CW00920432

AQA GCSE
English Language 8700

Illustrated revision and practice

Published by
PG Online Limited
The Old Coach House
35 Main Road
Tolpuddle
Dorset
DT2 7EW
United Kingdom

sales@pgonline.co.uk
www.clearrevise.com
www.pgonline.co.uk
2022

PG ONLINE

PREFACE

Absolute clarity! That's the aim.

This is everything you need to ace your English Language exams and beam with pride. Each exam question is laid out in a beautifully illustrated format that is clear, approachable and as concise and simple as possible.

The checklist on the contents pages will help you keep track of what you have already worked through and what's left before the big day.

We have included worked exam-style questions with answers. There is also a set of exam-style questions at the end of each section for you to practise writing answers. You can check your answers against those given at the end of the book.

LEVELS OF LEARNING

Based on the degree to which you are able to truly understand a new topic, we recommend that you work in stages. Start by reading a short explanation of something, then try and recall what you've just read. This will have limited effect if you stop there but it aids the next stage. Question everything. Write down your own summary and then complete and mark a related exam-style question. Cover up the answers if necessary but learn from them once you've seen them. Lastly, teach someone else. Explain the topic in a way that they can understand. Have a go at the different practice questions – they offer an insight into how and where marks are awarded.

Design and artwork: Jessica Webb / PG Online Ltd
Graphics / images: © Shutterstock

First edition 2022   10 9 8 7 6 5 4 3 2 1
A catalogue entry for this book is available from the British Library
ISBN: 978-1-910523-41-4

Printed on FSC certified paper by Bell and Bain Ltd, Glasgow, UK.

THE SCIENCE OF REVISION

Illustrations and words

Research has shown that revising with words and pictures doubles the quality of responses by students.[1] This is known as 'dual-coding' because it provides two ways of fetching the information from our brain. The improvement in responses is particularly apparent in students when they are asked to apply their knowledge to different problems. Recall, application and judgement are all specifically and carefully assessed in public examination questions.

Retrieval of information

Retrieval practice encourages students to come up with answers to questions.[2] The closer the question is to one you might see in a real examination, the better. Also, the closer the environment in which a student revises is to the 'examination environment', the better. Students who had a test 2–7 days away did 30% better using retrieval practice than students who simply read, or repeatedly reread material. Students who were expected to teach the content to someone else after their revision period did better still.[3] What was found to be most interesting in other studies is that students using retrieval methods and testing for revision were also more resilient to the introduction of stress.[4]

Ebbinghaus' forgetting curve and spaced learning

Ebbinghaus' 140-year-old study examined the rate at which we forget things over time. The findings still hold true. However, the act of forgetting facts and techniques and relearning them is what cements them into the brain.[5] Spacing out revision is more effective than cramming – we know that, but students should also know that the space between revisiting material should vary depending on how far away the examination is. A cyclical approach is required. An examination 12 months away necessitates revisiting covered material about once a month. A test in 30 days should have topics revisited every 3 days – intervals of roughly a tenth of the time available.[6]

Summary

Students: the more tests and past questions you do, in an environment as close to examination conditions as possible, the better you are likely to perform on the day. If you prefer to listen to music while you revise, tunes without lyrics will be far less detrimental to your memory and retention. Silence is most effective.[5] If you choose to study with friends, choose carefully – effort is contagious.[7]

1. Mayer, R. E., & Anderson, R. B. (1991). Animations need narrations: An experimental test of dual-coding hypothesis. *Journal of Education Psychology*, (83)4, 484–490.

2. Roediger III, H. L., & Karpicke, J.D. (2006). Test-enhanced learning: Taking memory tests improves long-term retention. *Psychological Science*, 17(3), 249–255.

3. Nestojko, J., Bui, D., Kornell, N. & Bjork, E. (2014). Expecting to teach enhances learning and organisation of knowledge in free recall of text passages. *Memory and Cognition*, 42(7), 1038–1048.

4. Smith, A. M., Floerke, V. A., & Thomas, A. K. (2016) Retrieval practice protects memory against acute stress. *Science*, 354(6315), 1046–1048.

5. Perham, N., & Currie, H. (2014). Does listening to preferred music improve comprehension performance? *Applied Cognitive Psychology*, 28(2), 279–284.

6. Cepeda, N. J., Vul, E., Rohrer, D., Wixted, J. T. & Pashler, H. (2008). Spacing effects in learning a temporal ridgeline of optimal retention. *Psychological Science*, 19(11), 1095–1102.

7. Busch, B. & Watson, E. (2019), *The Science of Learning*, 1st ed. Routledge.

CONTENTS

☑

Structuring your answers..vi ☐
Technical accuracy ....viii ☐
Assessment objectives (AOs)...xii ☐

Paper 1   Explorations in creative reading and writing

☑

1, A   Exam text..2 ☐
1, A   Reading the text..3 ☐
1, A   Question 1 — Exam technique..4 ☐
1, A   Question 1 — Examination practice...6 ☐
1, A   Question 2 — Exam technique..7 ☐
1, A   Question 2 — Words and phrases..8 ☐
1, A   Question 2 — Language features and techniques..11 ☐
1, A   Question 2 — Sentence forms..14 ☐
1, A   Question 2 — Examination practice...17 ☐
1, A   Question 3 — Exam technique..18 ☐
1, A   Question 3 — Structural forms...19 ☐
1, A   Question 3 — Examination practice...24 ☐
1, A   Question 4 — Exam technique..25 ☐
1, A   Question 4 — Examination practice...28 ☐
1, B   Question 5 — Exam technique..29 ☐
1, B   Question 5 — Writing a plan...30 ☐
1, B   Question 5 — Writing stories..31 ☐
1, B   Question 5 — Writing descriptions...32 ☐
1, B   Question 5 — Examination practice...36 ☐

Paper 2   Writers' viewpoints and perspectives

☑

2, A   Exam texts...38 ☐
2, A   19th-century texts...39 ☐
2, A   Audience..41 ☐
2, A   Purpose..42 ☐
2, A   Question 1 — Exam technique..43 ☐
2, A   Question 1 — Examination practice...45 ☐
2, A   Question 2 — Exam technique..46 ☐
2, A   Question 2 — Examination practice...49 ☐

2, A	Question 3 — Exam technique	50	☐
2, A	**Question 3 — Examination practice**	**52**	☐
2, A	Question 4 — Exam technique	53	☐
2, A	Question 4 — Writers' attitudes	54	☐
2, A	**Question 4 — Examination practice**	**58**	☐
2, B	Question 5 — Exam technique	60	☐
2, B	Question 5 — Writing a plan	61	☐
2, B	Question 5 — Articles	62	☐
2, B	Question 5 — Letters	63	☐
2, B	Question 5 — Speeches	64	☐
2, B	**Question 5 — Examination practice**	**67**	☐

Examination practice answers	68	
Levels-based mark schemes for extended response questions	73	
Index	79	
Notes and doodles	81	
Examination tips	**83**	

MARK ALLOCATIONS

Green mark allocations[1] on answers to in-text questions throughout this guide help to indicate where marks are gained within the answers. A bracketed '1' e.g. [1] = one valid point worthy of a mark. There are often many more points to make than there are marks available so you have more opportunity to max out your answers than you may think.

Higher mark questions require extended responses. These answers should be marked as a whole in accordance with the levels of response guidance on **pages 73-78**.

Understanding the paper reference tabs

This number refers to the exam paper. In this case, Paper 2.

This number refers to the section of the exam paper. In this case, Section A.

2, A

STRUCTURING YOUR ANSWERS

For the longer response questions across both papers, you need to know how to structure your answers.

PEEDL

Use **PEEDL** to help structure your longer-response answers and link them back to the question. PEEDL stands for **point**, **evidence**, **explanation**, **develop**, **link**.

1. **Point**: Make a point that answers the question.
2. **Evidence**: Use evidence from the text to support your point. This could be a direct quote or a paraphrased example (an example written in your own words). Try to use short quotes which clearly back up the point you're making.
3. **Explanation**: Explain how the evidence you've selected supports your point.
4. **Develop**: Include some additional information to make your point more detailed. You could consider the impact on the reader or give your opinion on how effective the writing is.
5. **Link**: Link your paragraph to the next point or back to the question.

You should clearly signal the explanation and develop parts to the examiner. You can do this by using phrases such as:

This suggests/implies/shows that...

This idea is developed by...

The effect of this is...

This alerts the reader that...

This is reinforced by...

The writer presents...

You might have been taught a different word, e.g. PEEL (point, example, evidence, link), but PEEDL reminds you to develop your point.

An example of how to use PEEDL

How does the writer use language to describe the mountain?

The writer uses language to suggest that the mountain is dangerous, for example the phrase "glinting wickedly". This use of personification suggests that the mountain is evil, and hints to the reader that something terrible will happen to the mountaineers. It is clear the writer uses language to make the reader feel apprehensive about the mountain.

This is the point...

...this is the evidence...

...this is the explanation...

...this is where the point is developed...

...and this is where the point is linked back to the question.

Make sure to use quote marks (also known as **inverted commas**) around any words taken directly from the text, and to copy the words exactly as they appear.

You should use PEEDL in questions 2, 3 and 4 on Paper 1, and questions 3 and 4 on Paper 2.

Paragraphs

Each PEEDL should have its own paragraph. You can signal a new paragraph by starting a new line, and either indenting the text or leaving an empty line above it.

Join your paragraphs with linking words to make your answer flow smoothly. For example, if you're adding extra points that agree with or extend your previous point, you could use:

Firstly / Secondly / Thirdly / Finally...   Furthermore...   Another way that...   In addition...

If your next point presents an alternative view, you could use:

However...   Whereas...   Alternatively...   On the other hand...   Contrastingly...

As well as being grammatically correct, using paragraphs makes it easier for the examiner to follow your answer and see where you're starting a new point.

You also need to use paragraphs in fiction writing. You should start a new paragraph when a new character speaks, or if the setting, time or place of the narrative changes. For more about fiction writing, look at **pages 31–33**.

Correcting paragraphs

If you've forgotten to start a new paragraph, you can add two forward slashes (//) to signal where a new paragraph should go:

... this shows that the narrator is fearful of what might happen. // Another way that the writer creates a tense atmosphere is by....

Make sure you use correct spelling, punctuation and grammar in your answers (**pages viii–xi**).

TECHNICAL ACCURACY

It's important that all your answers are well written, but it's extra-important for Q5 on both papers because there are 16 marks available for technical accuracy.

Sentences

Make sure all your sentences start with a capital letter, and end with a full stop (or an exclamation mark or question mark).

Don't over-use exclamation marks and never put more than one exclamation mark at the end of a sentence.

 As well as demonstrating that you can use correct spelling, punctuation and grammar, you'll also be marked on how varied it is, so to get the top marks, try to use a range of different techniques.

Punctuation

Make sure you know how to use basic punctuation correctly.

Apostrophes

Apostrophes show where letters are missing from words. For example, the apostrophe in 'didn't' shows that there's an 'o' missing from 'did not'.

Apostrophes can also show that something belongs to someone. For example, 'Milly's bag' or 'Raj's laptop'. If you want to show that something belongs to more than one person or thing, put the apostrophe after the 's', e.g. 'the cats' food bowls'.

Make sure you know the difference between 'it's' and 'its'. 'It's' is the shortened version of 'it is' or 'it has' whereas 'its' means 'belonging to it'.

Commas

Commas can separate items in a list.	The cellar was dark, dank and dingy.
Commas can separate extra information in a sentence. If the information in between the commas can be removed and the sentence still makes sense, the commas have been used correctly.	Alex, who had just turned 17, desperately wanted a car.
Commas go after **fronted adverbials**. Fronted adverbials are phrases that appear at the start of a sentence and act like adverbs. Often they can be moved to the end of the sentence and the sentence will still make sense.	<u>After a thorough search of the park</u>, the dog turned up safe and well. The dog turned up safe and well <u>after a thorough search of the park</u>.

Direct speech

If you include direct speech in your creative writing, make sure to punctuate it correctly.

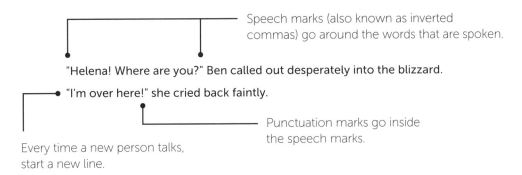

Speech marks (also known as inverted commas) go around the words that are spoken.

"Helena! Where are you?" Ben called out desperately into the blizzard.

"I'm over here!" she cried back faintly.

Punctuation marks go inside the speech marks.

Every time a new person talks, start a new line.

Colons

Colons can be used to introduce a list.	Sarah checked her knapsack: a coil of rope, an ice axe, three blankets and a book of matches.
Colons can also be used to introduce an explanation.	He knew the house wasn't secure: he had left the door unlocked.

Semi-colons

Semi-colons separate longer items in a list.	Sarah checked her knapsack: a coil of rope that was sturdy and undamaged; an ice axe that she had recently sharpened; three thick wool blankets; and an unused book of matches.
Semi-colons also join two sentences together where the sentences are about the same thing and make sense by themselves.	Jules is going on holiday to Spain; Tyson is going on holiday to Greece.

Ellipsis

Ellipsis is three dots grouped together, e.g. '...'. It can be used in direct speech to show a long pause, that someone has been interrupted or that their speech tails off.	"I'm not accusing you of stealing, it's just..." the shopkeeper said meekly, pointing to the chocolate bar sticking out of the customer's pocket.

The examiner will be impressed if you can use more complex punctuation, like ellipsis, colons and semi-colons, but only if you can use them correctly and appropriately.

Standard English

Your writing should be in **Standard English**. This is the form of English that most people agree is correct. You should avoid using **slang** or **informal language**.

- ⊖ He was proper chuffed that he won the award.
- ⊕ He was delighted that he won the award.

Make sure you haven't used any **double negatives** because they're grammatically incorrect.

- ⊖ He never did nothing.
- ⊕ He never did anything.   ⊕ He always did nothing.

> The only time you might want to use non-Standard English is if a character in a story you're writing speaks with an accent. Only attempt to use non-Standard English if you're confident you can pull it off.

Editing

You should leave some time at the end of the exam to double-check what you've written. As well as correcting any mistakes, you can use this time to edit your work to make sure that your writing flows smoothly, clearly answers the question and any unnecessary sentences have been trimmed.

Spelling

When you're writing under pressure it's easy to make silly spelling mistakes.
- Watch out for words like 'there', 'their' and 'they're' that sound the same but are spelt differently depending on the context.
- Don't spell 'should have', 'could have' or 'would have' as 'should of', 'could of' or 'would of'.

> Learn how to spell tricky technical terms like 'metaphor', 'simile' and 'onomatopoeia', so you can spell them confidently in the exam.

Vocabulary

To get top marks in technical accuracy you need to demonstrate that you have a good vocabulary and can use it appropriately. Make sure you use a variety of words, and avoid using unoriginal language such as 'nice' and 'said'.

- ⊖ The hotel was nice. It had a nice pool and a nice view from the balcony.
- ⊕ The hotel was incredible. It had an amazing pool and a stunning view from the balcony.

Paragraphs

You should start a new paragraph (by starting a new line and leaving an indent or an empty line above) each time:

fiction writing

- a different character speaks.
- the action moves to a different place.
- the action moves to a different time.

non-fiction writing

- you make a new point

Grammar

Make sure you use **tenses** consistently in your writing. Don't write half your story in the present tense, and then switch to the past tense for no reason.

- ⊖ The house was falling down and hasn't been lived in for years.
- ⊕ The house was falling down and hadn't been lived in for years.

Make sure that all your **subjects** and **pronouns** agree with their verbs.

- ⊖ They was
- ⊕ They were
- ⊖ He were
- ⊕ He was
- ⊖ They is
- ⊕ They are
- ⊖ She are
- ⊕ She is

Correcting mistakes

It's likely that you'll make some mistakes in your writing, so make sure you know how to correct errors neatly and carefully.

If you've spelt something incorrectly, carefully cross out the word and rewrite the correction above it.	There ~~Their~~ was no doubt the wheel was broken.
If you've missed out a word, use this symbol ^ where the missing word should go, and write the word above it.	crept She ^ along quietly.
If you've forgotten to start a new paragraph, just put **//** where you want the new paragraph to start.	...and he fell asleep. **//** The next day, he awoke with a start.

Leave at least five minutes at the end of the exam to read over your answer to Q5. Editing your answer and correcting mistakes could greatly increase your marks.

ASSESSMENT OBJECTIVES

In the exam, your answers will be marked against assessment objectives (AOs). It's important you understand which skills each AO tests.

AO1

- Find and understand information and ideas from text(s). The information could be stated clearly, or implied.
- Choose and combine evidence from different texts.

The AOs on this page have been written in simple language. See the AQA website for the official wording.

AO2

- Explain, comment on, and analyse how writers use language and structure to achieve effects and influence readers.
- Use relevant technical terms to support your answer.

AO3

- Compare writers' ideas and attitudes, and how they are expressed, across two or more texts.

AO4

- Evaluate texts critically and support evaluations with appropriate evidence from the texts.

AO5

- Write clearly, effectively and imaginatively. Use an appropriate tone, style and register for different forms, purposes and audiences.
- Use structural and grammatical features to organise your answers.

AO6

- Use a range of vocabulary and sentence structures for clarity, purpose and effect, with accurate spelling and punctuation.

AOs 7–9 aren't included on this page, but they test the spoken language element of the course. See the AQA website for more information.

PAPER 1

Explorations in creative reading and writing

Information about Paper 1

Written exam: 1 hour 45 minutes
80 marks
Q1–5 are mandatory
You will have a choice of two questions for Q5.
50% of the qualification grade

Specification coverage

Section A will test AO1, AO2 and AO4
Section B will test AO5 and AO6

Questions

One short-form question, two longer form questions
and two extended-writing questions.

EXAM TEXT

Paper 1 is split into two sections: Section A and Section B. All the questions in Section A will be about an unseen fiction extract.

What to expect from the exam text

Text type

The extract will be from a **literary fiction** text written in the 20th or 21st century (i.e. from 1900-present day). It might be taken from the beginning, middle or end of a longer text. The extract will be **unseen** which means you won't have studied it before the exam.

Literary fiction just means a well-written fiction text.

Purpose

The purpose of literary fiction is to **entertain**, so the extract will have been written to make you feel certain emotions and to keep you interested in the story. Some of the questions in Section A will ask you to comment on how successfully the writer has achieved this.

Subject and genre

The text could be about anything and from any **genre** (i.e. adventure, mystery, historical fiction).

The extract will be printed in a separate booklet so it's easier to refer to in the exam.

Word count

The text will be between 700–800 words. The extract will probably be printed across multiple pages, and the phrase "end of source" will indicate where the extract finishes.

Introduction

There will be a couple of sentences at the start of the extract which will briefly introduce the **setting** and **characters**. It will mention who wrote the text and when.

Line numbers

The line numbers down the left-hand side of the page can be used to navigate the text. Some of the questions will use line numbers to specify which part of the text you need to take your answer from.

Glossary

A couple of difficult or unusual words might be defined at the end of the text, but don't rely on this.

READING THE TEXT

All the questions in Paper 1, Section A will be about the extract, so it's really important you understand the text before you start writing.

Reading the text

Read through the questions first. This will help you stay focused when you read the extract. Read the text quickly, but carefully. Don't just skim read. If you read too quickly, you might miss something or misunderstand what's happening. It's better to spend a few extra minutes reading the text to make sure you really understand it.

You can write on the extract, so underline or note down anything that could help you answer the questions, such as examples of literary techniques (see **pages 11–12**). Once you're ready to start writing your answers, make sure you keep referring back to the text.

You should spend about 15 minutes reading the source and questions at the start of the exam.

Don't ignore the introductory sentences above the text. There could be some information to help you understand the characters or context.

Effect of the text on you as the reader

After you've read the text, think about the effect the writer was trying to create on you as a reader. Most fiction writers want to entertain the reader to make sure they keep reading, but they might do this in different ways. For example, the extract in the exam might:

- **make the reader feel a certain emotion** — excitement, disgust, fear, sadness.
- **develop a character** — to make a character more interesting, more relatable or make the reader more invested in their story. The main character in a story is the **protagonist**.
- **develop the story** — to keep the plot moving so the reader doesn't lose interest.
- **use vivid descriptions** — to create a clear picture in the reader's mind of a character or setting, so the reader is more absorbed in the story.
- **create tension** — to make the text exciting to keep the reader invested and interested.

The purpose of literary fiction is to entertain, but non-fiction texts may have different purposes. There's more on **page 42** about the purposes of non-fiction texts.

QUESTION 1 – EXAM TECHNIQUE

The first question in the exam tests your ability to spot **explicit information** (facts that have been directly stated in the extract).

Example question

01   Read the first part of the source, from **lines 1 to 5**.

List **four** things about the house from this part of the source.   **[4 marks]**

In the exam, you'll get a full extract to answer the question. This is just a sample question to show you the question wording you can expect.

How to answer question 1

- This question tests the first part of AO1 (see **page xii** for the AOs). You need to find and understand information from the text.

- Make sure you take your answers from the part of the text specified by the line numbers. If you take your answers from any other part of the source, you won't get the marks.

- Your answers should only refer to the thing or person stated in the question. In the example above, only answers which refer to the house will be awarded marks.

- There are usually more than four correct answers, but you only need to write down four. Writing extra answers won't get you any more marks.

- It's fine to write down the most obvious answers. You won't get extra marks for spotting something someone else hasn't, and you shouldn't need to **infer** (read between the lines) information from the text.

- You will be awarded one mark per correct answer.

- You can either quote directly from the text or use your own words.

- Your answers don't have to be in full sentences.

- You should spend about 4 minutes on this question.

This extract is taken from the beginning of a novel called *The Secret Garden*. The main character, Mary, has just woken up in an unfamiliar room.

1. The walls were covered with tapestry with a forest scene embroidered on it. There were fantastically dressed people under the trees and in the distance there was a glimpse of the turrets of a castle. There were hunters and horses and dogs and ladies. Mary felt as if she were in the forest with them. Out of a deep window she could see a great climbing stretch of land
5. which seemed to have no trees on it, and to look rather like an endless, dull, purplish sea.

Read the first part of the source, from **lines 1 to 5**.

List **four** things about the tapestry from this part of the source.   [4 marks]

1. *The tapestry is on the wall.*[1]
2. *The tapestry has a forest scene on it.*[1]
3. *The tapestry has a castle on it.*[1]
4. *The tapestry has dogs on it.*[1]

There are more than four things you could write about the tapestry, but you only need to mention 4 to get the marks. Starting each sentence with "The tapestry..." helps to keep this answer focused on the specific item in the question.

EXAMINATION PRACTICE

1. The great spider was lying asleep when the Lion found him, and it looked so ugly that
    its foe turned up his nose in disgust. Its legs were quite as long as the tiger had said, and
    its body covered with coarse black hair. It had a great mouth, with a row of sharp teeth
    a foot long; but its head was joined to the pudgy body by a neck as slender as a
5. wasp's waist.
    This gave the Lion a hint of the best way to attack the creature, and as he knew it was
    easier to fight it asleep than awake, he gave a great spring and landed directly upon the
    monster's back. Then, with one blow of his heavy paw, all armed with sharp claws, he
    knocked the spider's head from its body. Jumping down, he watched it until the long
10. legs stopped wiggling, when he knew it was quite dead.

1. Read **lines 1 to 5**. List **four** things about the spider.   **[4 marks]**

1. The storeroom was a damp chamber in what had been the old farmhouse. There was
    no carpet on the uneven floor. It was black as pitch, for the windows were heavily
    shuttered. I made out by groping that the walls were lined with boxes and barrels and
    sacks of some heavy stuff. The whole place smelt of mould and disuse.
5. My jailer turned the key in the door, and I could hear them shifting their feet as they
    stood on guard outside.
    I sat down in that chilly darkness in a very miserable frame of mind.

2. Read **lines 1 to 4**. List **four** things about the storeroom.   **[4 marks]**

1. The sled was without runners. It was made of stout birch-bark, and its full surface rested
    on the snow. The front end of the sled was turned up, like a scroll, in order to force
    down and under the bore of soft snow that surged like a wave before it. On the sled,
    securely lashed, was a long and narrow oblong box.
5. In advance of the dogs, on wide snowshoes, toiled a man. At the rear of the sled toiled
    a second man.

3. Read **lines 1 to 4**. List **four** things about the sled.   **[4 marks]**

QUESTION 2 – EXAM TECHNIQUE

Question 2 tests your ability to analyse a writer's use of language and sentence forms, and their effect on the reader.

Example question

02   Look in detail at the extract from **lines 14 to 23**.

How does the writer use language to describe Meg?

You could include the writer's choice of:
- words and phrases
- language features and techniques
- sentence forms

[8 marks]

In the exam, you'll get a full extract to answer the question. This is just a sample question to show you the question wording you can expect.

How to answer question 2

- This question covers the language part of AO2 (see **page xii**). It tests how well you can understand **implicit information**, i.e. information that is not directly stated in the text.

- Make sure you refer to the part of the extract stated by the line numbers. The correct section of text will probably be printed above the question on the exam paper.

- Your answers should only refer to the thing or person specified in the question. In the example above, only answers that refer to Meg will be awarded marks.

- You don't need to write something for every bullet point. It can be tricky to write something meaningful about sentence forms, so it's fine to focus on language instead.

- Make sure you provide examples from the text to support your points.

- It's not enough to just spot techniques. You must comment on the effect on reader too.

- This question is worth 8 marks. You should spend about 9 minutes on it.

- You will need to reference the text in your answer. For more advice on using evidence from a text, see **page vi**.

When commenting on the effect on the reader, avoid generic and vague comments such as, "it grabs the reader's attention". Make sure your inferences are specific to the text and the effect the author is trying to create.

QUESTION 2 – WORDS AND PHRASES

The first bullet point of question 2 asks you to comment on the writer's choice of words and phrases. When you comment on words and phrases, make sure you always link your answers back to the effect on the reader.

Word types

Words can be grouped into different categories depending on their function in a sentence. You should use the correct terminology to refer to word types in your answers.

Nouns

Nouns are naming words that refer to people, places, things or ideas, e.g. 'Malik', 'Bristol', 'cat', 'hope'. **Proper nouns** (e.g. a country or someone's name) always start with a capital letter.

Pronouns

Pronouns replace nouns in sentences, e.g. 'I', 'he', 'she', 'they'.

Pronouns tell you whether a text is written in the **first**, **second** or **third person** (see **page 20**).

Adjectives

Adjectives describe nouns, e.g. 'bright', 'beautiful', 'red'.

Adverbs

Adverbs describe verbs, e.g. 'quickly', 'happily', 'purposefully'.

Verbs

Verbs are action words, e.g. 'walk', 'shouted', 'singing'. Verbs can tell you what **tense** a text is written in:

- Verbs ending in '-ed', e.g. 'shouted', 'walked', 'danced' are usually in the **past** tense.
- Verbs ending in '-(e)s', e.g. 'goes', 'plays', 'dreams' and verbs with 'is' and ending in '-ing', e.g. 'is following', 'is writing' are usually in the **present** tense.
- Verbs with 'will' before them, e.g. 'will travel', 'will visit' are usually in the **future** tense.

Some verbs are **irregular**, and don't follow the rules above. For example, 'was' is in the past tense, but it doesn't end with '-ed'.

Determiners

Determiners, e.g. 'the', 'that', 'a' or 'an', usually appear before nouns, and tell you whether something is specific ('that banana') or non-specific ('a banana').

There are other word types, but these are the most common.

As well as thinking about what each word means individually, think about how an author combines different word types in their writing to build an effect. For example, 'frenzy', 'screamed', 'frightening' and 'violently' are all different word types, but they create a feeling of alarm.

Tone

Fiction texts often have a **tone**. This is the mood or atmosphere that the author is trying to create, e.g., tense, scary, calming. The tone can change throughout the story or extract, depending on how the writer wants the reader to feel. Writers can achieve different tones by using words and phrases (see below) as well as sentence forms (**pages 14–15**) and structural techniques (**pages 19–21**).

Words and phrases

Writers are very deliberate about the words and phrases they use. They will have chosen words that make the reader feel a certain way.

Connotations

Connotations are the deeper meanings of words. For example, 'walk' and 'amble' have similar meanings, but 'amble' has connotations of someone moving slowly or without purpose. If a character 'ambles' they might be unhurried or lazy.

Recognising connotations can help you comment on implicit information, which you need to do for AO1.

Repetition

When a writer repeats a significant word or phrase, it is usually done deliberately to reinforce the tone or theme (see **page 12**).

> Everything was still. The river, shallow and murky, was still. The long grass, usually buffeted this way and that, was still. The air, oppressive and hot, was the most still of all.

The repetition of the word 'still' fills the reader with suspense. They want to know why the scene is so still.

Semantic field

Words with a similar meaning, or words which are related to the same topic, can be grouped into a semantic field. For example, 'charred', 'baked' and 'fried' are all from the semantic field of cooking, and the words create the feeling of being uncomfortably hot.

Emotive language

Emotive language describes words and phrases which provoke an emotional response from a reader.

> He chewed, gulped and slurped his meal noisily. Crumbs and spit flying from his mouth as he talked.

This description makes the reader feel disgust towards the character.

> Mist curled and lingered around the darkening forest, as shadows darted in between the branches.

This description makes the reader feel unsettled.

Remember, it's not enough to just spot techniques. You must be able to comment on the effect of the technique on the reader too, and these comments need to be specific and relevant. Vague and generic comments such as 'it makes the text interesting' aren't enough to get top marks.

This extract describes what a character, Dorothy, can see from her farmhouse.

When Dorothy stood in the doorway and looked around, she could see nothing but the great grey prairie on every side. Not a tree nor a house broke the broad sweep of flat country that reached to the edge of the sky in all directions. The sun had baked the ploughed land into a grey mass, with little cracks running through it. Even the grass was not green, for the sun had burned the tops of the long blades until they were the same grey colour to be seen everywhere. Once the house had been painted, but the sun blistered the paint and the rains washed it away, and now the house was as dull and grey as everything else.

How does the writer use words and phrases to describe the scene?

The writer uses words and phrases to describe the scene as being desolate and bleak. The repetition of the adjective "grey" presents the scene as colourless and has connotations of being dull and unwelcoming. This idea is developed further when the writer describes objects that once had colour, like the land, grass and the house, as being "baked", "burned" and "blistered" until they turned grey. These verbs are from the semantic field of being 'charred', which reinforces the idea that it is an inhospitable and destructive environment where anything colourful is scorched and has the colour burned off it. This creates a hopeless tone, and makes the reader feel sympathy towards Dorothy.

The writer also presents the scene as being inescapable. The text says that the land "reached to the edge of the sky in all directions" which suggests that it is endless. This implies that Dorothy is trapped somewhere inhospitable, which makes the reader feel anxious for her and presents the scene as oppressive and hopeless.

This answer should be marked in accordance with the levels-based mark scheme on page 73.

This example answer only focuses on words and phrases. The question in the exam will also ask about language features (**page 11–13**) and sentence forms (**page 14–16**).

QUESTION 2 – LANGUAGE FEATURES AND TECHNIQUES

To get good marks in question 2, you need to know the names of linguistic techniques, how to spot them and what effect they have on the reader.

Language techniques

Sensory language

Sensory language describes words and phrases which appeal to one or more of the readers' senses, e.g. sight, smell, taste, touch and hearing. Sensory language helps the reader to use their own experiences to clearly picture what the writer is describing.

 Sight: 'Open petals were scattered with twinkling droplets of dew.'

 Smell: 'A rotten, putrid mound of manure festered in the sun.'

 Taste: 'She bit into the crisp, sour apple.'

 Touch: 'Snuggled under fleece blankets, Lisa felt the soft, plush fabric on her toes.'

 Hearing: 'The branches tapped briskly on the windowpane.'

Alliteration

Alliteration describes words near each other starting with the same sound. Alliteration makes a phrase leap out at the reader and makes it more memorable. Different letters create different sounds which can create distinct moods, for example, an 's' sound is soft and hissing, whereas 't' can sound harsh and abrupt.

> Shining softly, the street lamp signalled safety.

> Be careful when identifying alliteration because the sound the letters make needs to be the same. Although the sentence 'The gnome glared at the giant' repeats the letter 'g', none of the words start with the same sound, so this is not an example of alliteration.

Onomatopoeia

Onomatopoeia is a technique where words sound like the sound they are describing, e.g. 'buzz', 'miaow', 'bang'. Onomatopoeia makes it easy for the reader to imagine the sound.

 You should always say what effect a technique has on a reader, and make sure your comments are specific and relevant to the text. Avoid vague comments like "it grabs the reader's attention". Instead, think about the specific emotion the writer is trying to make you feel.

Figurative language

Figurative language is language used in a **non-literal** way. Figurative language helps to create a clear image in the reader's mind by comparing a person or object to something the reader would recognise. For example:

Similes

Similes describe something 'like' or 'as' something else.

> The sun was like a burnished medallion.

Metaphors

Metaphors describe something as being something else.

> The boy was a wolf, tearing at the food in front of him.

Personification

Personification describes something non-human using human qualities.

> The chair sighed with dissatisfaction as Gerald sat down.

Analogy

Analogy compares two things or ideas. As well as creating a memorable image, analogies can also make something easier to understand.

> The lake is roughly the size of four football pitches.

Theme, symbolism and motif

Theme

A **theme** is a text's central idea (or ideas). Writers can use texts to explore their feelings on certain themes, for example, love, guilt, nature etc.

Motif

Motif is an element (i.e. an image, phrase or situation) that repeats in a piece of fiction. For example, if a character often walks in the rain, it might suggest that they are miserable or unlucky. Motifs add depth to a piece of writing, and can help reinforce the text's theme.

Symbolism

Symbolism is when an author uses a symbol to represent an idea. For example, blood might be used to symbolise danger, or a teddy bear could symbolise childhood. Symbolism can be more effective than the writer describing something in detail.

For example, the image of a teddy bear left in the rain conjures images of abandonment and loss of childhood more effectively than a description could.

Identifying 'big ideas' in a text can help you achieve top marks in the exam. It proves to the examiner that you understand the deeper meaning of the text.

This extract describes a fight between two dogs, Spitz and Buck.

They rolled over and over in the powdery snow. Spitz gained his feet almost as though he had not been overthrown, slashing Buck down the shoulder and leaping clear. Twice his teeth clipped together, like the steel jaws of a trap, as he backed away for better footing, with lean and lifting lips that writhed and snarled.
In a flash Buck knew it. The time had come. It was to the death. As they circled about, snarling, ears laid back, keenly watchful for the advantage, the scene came to Buck with a sense of familiarity. He seemed to remember it all,—the white woods, and earth, and moonlight, and the thrill of battle. Over the whiteness and silence brooded a ghostly calm. There was not the faintest whisper of air— nothing moved, not a leaf quivered, the visible breaths of the dogs rising slowly and lingering in the frosty air.

How does the writer use language features and techniques to describe the fight between the dogs?

The writer uses language to describe the fight between the two dogs as intense and vicious. The author achieves this by using onomatopoeic words "clipped" and "snarled". This use of sensory language helps the reader to clearly imagine the ferocious biting sounds made by the dogs. The imagery of the dogs biting is further emphasised by the simile "like the steel jaws of a trap" to describe the dog's mouth. This phrase implies the dog's teeth are sharp and deadly, and when he bites, his grip will be savage.

The author also uses alliteration in the phrase "lean and lifting lips". This repetition of the 'l' sound draws the reader's attention to the dog's snarl, and the sensory imagery reinforces the cruelty of its mouth. This makes the reader fearful that one or both dogs will be badly hurt.

This answer should be marked in accordance with the levels-based mark scheme on page 73.

This extract only focuses on language features and techniques. The question in the exam will also ask about words and phrases (**pages 8–9**) and sentence forms (**pages 14–15**).

QUESTION 2 – SENTENCE FORMS

It's not just language you need to analyse in question 2, you also need to comment on how words are put into sentences, and what effect they have.

Sentence function

Sentences have four main functions:

1. **Statements** give the reader information. | The house was built on the hill.

2. **Questions** ask the character (or reader) something. | Where does Lady Fellows live?

3. **Exclamations** show strong emotions, for example anger, delight, fear etc. They usually start with 'what' or 'how' and end with an exclamation mark. | What a mess this is!

4. **Commands** tell the reader to do something. They often start with **imperative verbs** (verbs that give an instruction). | Go upstairs and tidy your room.

> Questions in non-fiction texts are usually directed at the reader and are **rhetorical** (i.e. don't require an answer). Even if they don't require an answer, rhetorical questions encourage the reader to think what their answer might be. (See **page 56**.)

Sentence length

Short sentences

Short sentences can increase the pace of a piece of writing to create tension or a feeling of panic, confusion or excitement.

> He ran. Quicker and quicker. His legs burning. His lungs bursting.

Long sentences

Long sentences slow the pace of a text. They can create the feeling of time moving gradually or a feeling of laziness or comfort.

> Camilla fetched the kettle, filled it with water, and set it on the stovetop. Daylight was streaming through the windows and soft breeze fluttered at the curtains, as the kettle merrily bubbled away.

As well as learning about sentence forms to help you answer question 2 on Paper 1, you should look to incorporate different sentence forms in your responses to question 5 on Papers 1 and 2.

Sentence structure

Sentences usually contain a **subject** (the person or thing performing the action), a **verb** (the action word) and an **object** (the thing having the action done to it). Most sentences are written in this order, and this is known as the active voice.

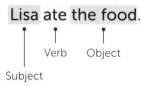

Lisa ate the food.

    Verb   Object

Subject

The **passive voice** is when the object of a sentence, becomes the subject of a sentence. The verb form is put in the past tense with 'was' or 'is'. The passive makes a text sound less personal, because it's not always clear who is doing the action.

The food was eaten (by Lisa).

Subject   Verb   Object

Sentences contain **clauses**. Clauses are made up of a **subject** and a **verb**. Different sentence structures contain different numbers and types of clauses:

Simple sentences usually contain one clause.	Hayden broke his finger.
Compound sentences contain two clauses which are usually joined with a **conjunction** (a joining word like 'and', 'but', 'so' etc). Both clauses need to make sense independently.	Hayden broke his finger in two places and his palm had been badly grazed.
Complex sentences have two or more clauses, but only one of the clauses makes sense by itself. In this example, 'After the accident' doesn't make sense by itself.	After the accident, Hayden's finger was broken.
Inversion is when a writer reorders a sentence to draw the reader's attention to the start of the sentence.	A bad graze was on Hayden's palm.

If you're struggling to write something meaningful about sentence forms, focus on language choices instead. You won't lose marks for ignoring sentence forms.

This extract is from *Peter Pan*. A pirate, Captain Hook, has captured a girl called Wendy, but he is interrupted by a crocodile coming on board his ship.

Hook smiled at them with his teeth closed, and he took a step toward Wendy. But he never reached her, he never heard the cry of anguish he hoped to wring from her. He heard something else instead.

It was the terrible tick-tick of the crocodile.

Very frightful was it to see the change that came over him. It was as if he had been clipped at every joint. He fell in a little heap.

The sound came steadily nearer; and in advance of it came this ghastly thought, "The crocodile is about to board the ship!"

How does the writer use sentence forms to describe the scene?

The writer uses sentence forms to show that Hook is frightened of the crocodile, and to build tension for the reader. In the first three sentences of the text, the clauses begin with the pronoun "he". This repetitive structure hints that Hook's response to the crocodile will be the focus of this passage, and it builds tension because the reader wants to know what Hook's reaction will be.

The writer uses sentence inversion to show just how frightened Hook is of the crocodile. Starting the sentence with "Very frightful" focuses the reader's attention on these words to emphasise the fear on the ship, and makes the reader feel anxious about what is going to happen.

The extract ends with the exclamation, "The crocodile is about to board the ship!". The exclamation suggests the strong emotion in this sentence, and reinforces the panic felt by the characters. This simple sentence also makes it very clear to the reader that the something exciting is going to happen when the crocodile comes aboard.

This answer should be marked in accordance with the levels-based mark scheme on page 73.

This extract only focuses on sentence forms. The question in the exam will also ask about words and phrases (**pages 8–9**) and language features (**pages 11–12**).

EXAMINATION PRACTICE

> They had driven over the crest of a hill. Below them was a pond, looking almost like a river so long and winding was it. A bridge spanned it midway and from there to its lower end, where an amber-hued belt of sand-hills shut it in from the dark blue gulf beyond, the water was a glory of many shifting hues—the most spiritual shadings of crocus and rose and ethereal green, with other elusive tintings for which no name has ever been found. Above the bridge the pond ran up into fringing groves of fir and maple and lay all darkly translucent in their wavering shadows. Here and there a wild plum leaned out from the bank like a white-clad girl tip-toeing to her own reflection. From the marsh at the head of the pond came the clear, mournfully-sweet chorus of the frogs. There was a little grey house peering around a white apple orchard on a slope beyond and, although it was not yet quite dark, a light was shining from one of its windows.

1. Look in detail at the extract above.

    How does the writer use language here to describe the scene?

    You could include writers' choice of:
    - words and phrases
    - language features and techniques
    - sentence forms   **[8 marks]**

> In the middle of the kitchen stood a long table of plain boards placed on trestles, with benches down each side. At one end of it, where an arm-chair stood pushed back, were spread the remains of the Badger's plain but ample supper. Rows of spotless plates winked from the shelves of the dresser at the far end of the room, and from the rafters overhead hung hams, bundles of dried herbs, nets of onions, and baskets of eggs. It seemed a place where heroes could fitly feast after victory, or where two or three friends of simple tastes could sit about as they pleased and eat and talk in comfort and contentment. The ruddy brick floor smiled up at the smoky ceiling; the oaken benches, shiny with long wear, exchanged cheerful glances with each other; plates on the dresser grinned at pots on the shelf, and the merry firelight flickered and played over everything without distinction.

2. Look in detail at the extract above.

    How does the writer use language here to describe the kitchen?

    You could include writers' choice of:
    - words and phrases
    - language features and techniques
    - sentence forms   **[8 marks]**

QUESTION 3 – EXAM TECHNIQUE

This question tests your ability to analyse a writer's use of **structure**. Think of structure like a camera on a movie set, focusing your attention on certain characters and information to help develop the plot.

> **03** You now need to think about the whole of the source.
>
> This text is from the beginning of a novel.
>
> How has the writer structured the text to interest you as a reader?
> You could write about:
> - what the writer focuses your attention on at the beginning of the source
> - how and why the writer changes this focus as the source develops
> - any other structural features that interest you   **[8 marks]**

In the exam, you'll get a full extract to answer the question. This is just a sample question to show you the question wording you can expect.

How to answer question 3

- This question covers the structure part of AO2 (see **page xii** for a list of the AOs). You need to explain, comment on and analyse how structure is used to achieve effects and influence readers.
- Make sure you look at the whole source.
- Don't just say that something "interests the reader and makes them want to read on". You've got to be specific and explain why it's interesting.
- It's not enough to just spot techniques either. You need to say how these techniques have been used and what the effect is on the reader.
- This question is worth 8 marks. You should spend about 9 minutes on it.

You'll need to use PEEDL to structure your answer. See **pages vi–vii** for more on using PEEDL.

QUESTION 3 – STRUCTURAL FORMS

Structure is how the author has ordered the text to reveal information about the characters and plot. Authors use different structures for different effects.

Chronological order

One of the simplest structures is **chronological order**. This just means putting events in time order (also called a **linear structure**). Most stories tend to follow a chronological order, but authors might add other techniques to make the structure more varied and interesting. Chronological order is easy for the reader to understand because the story is in a logical order.

Flashbacks and flashforwards

Sometimes authors add in **flashbacks** (something that has already happened) or **flashforwards** (something that is yet to happen). These techniques create a **non-chronological** (or **non-linear**) structure, where events don't happen in time order.

Flashbacks

Flashbacks can remind the reader about something they've already read or they can hint at something that's happened in the past. This can increase the tension in the story.

Flashforwards

Flashforwards can also be used to increase the tension. Mentioning something that is yet to happen makes the reader want to keep reading so they find out what happens. Flashforwards might also use **foreshadowing**, where something important is hinted at, but isn't fully explained.

Cinematic writing

Cinematic writing is a type of narrative that that's meant to mimic the experience of watching a film, think of the writer guiding your focus like a camera filming a movie. Cinematic writing focuses on characters' actions, rather than what they think.

Perspectives and narrators

Fiction texts always have a **narrative viewpoint**. This is the **perspective** the story is told from.

First-person narrator

A **first-person** narrator uses the pronouns 'I' and 'me'. The narrator is usually a character in the story.

First-person narrators tell their story directly to the reader, which helps the reader feel more involved in the action and creates a closer relationship between the narrator and reader.

> I always knew, that one day, I would be a star.

Second-person narrator

Second-person narrators are less common in fiction than first- and third-person narrators. They use the pronouns 'you'. Second-person narrators make the reader feel as though they are directly experiencing the events of the story.

> You always knew, that one day, you would be a star.

The second person is more common in non-fiction writing when a writer can use it to directly address an audience (see **page 54**).

Third-person narrator

A **third-person** narrator uses the pronouns 'he', 'she' and 'they'. Third-person narrators are more detached from the action, which can make the text more impersonal.

> He always knew, that one day, he would be a star.

Some third-person narrators are **omniscient**, i.e. they know what all the characters are thinking and feeling, whereas some third-person narrators are **limited narrators**, they only know what one character thinks and feels.

Narrative hook

A **narrative hook** is most commonly used at the start of a story or chapter. It could describe something exciting, gruesome, confusing or anything that provokes a strong reaction from a reader. Narrative hooks are written to grab a reader's attention and immerse them in the story.

> The phone call had come at 3.47 that morning, and it was the phone call that Chief Inspector Carlson had been dreading.

Remember it's not enough to just spot structural techniques. You need to consider why a writer has included them and what effect they are trying to create on the reader.

Cliffhangers

Cliffhangers tend to be used at the end of a story (or chapter). They describe events that are highly emotional (e.g. tense, scary, exciting, shocking), but the author doesn't resolve the action, instead the reader is left in suspense, wondering what will happen. A cliffhanger at the end of a chapter keeps the reader interested, and makes them want to continue with the story.

She reached for the door handle, and slowly turned it. She held her breath and swung the door open. What was waiting for her on the other side would change her life forever.

Climax

A **climax** is an important event in the story that the writer has been building up to. A story might have multiple, smaller climaxes, but there's usually a main climax that happens towards the end.

An **anti-climax** is when the story builds up to an exciting or important event, only to be disappointed by the resolution. Anti-climaxes can be used to create humour, suspense or frustration for the reader.

Juxtaposition

Juxtaposition is when two (or more) events are put next to each other, but the events provoke very different reactions. Provoking two extreme reactions from the reader can make the emotions feel even more intense.

On Friday, their beloved, cherished pet rabbit passed away peacefully.

On Saturday, Ceara prepared a delicious rabbit stew for her friends.

Speech

Direct speech (when characters talk to each other) can be used to reveal the plot and move the action along. Speech can also be used to tell the reader more about the character, or show the characters' thoughts and feelings about something. Speech allows the author to use the characters to reveal information to the reader instead of explaining it directly.

"Who's Daniel?" asked Lily.

"He's the man that's moved in next door." Justin lowered his voice slightly. "There's just something... unsettling about him."

As well as commenting on how the writer reveals information, consider if the writer is concealing anything from the reader to create tension or suspense.

 You should try to use some of these structural techniques in your answer to Paper 1, question 5.

This extract is from a short story called *La Dernière Mobilisation*, published in 1915.

On the left, the road comes up the hill out of a pool of mist; on the right it loses itself in the shadow of a wood. On the farther side of the highway a hedgerow, dusty in the moonlight, spreads an irregular border of black from the wood to the fog. Behind the hedgerow, slender poplar trees, evenly spaced, rule off the distance with inky lines.

A movement stirs the mist at the bottom of the hill. A monotonous rhythm grows in the silence. The mist darkens, and from it there emerges a strange shadowy column that reaches slowly up the hill, moving in silence to the sombre and muffled beating of a drum. As it draws nearer the shadow becomes two files of marching men bearing between them a long dim burden.

The leaders advance into the moonlight. Each two men are carrying between them a pole, and from pole to pole have been slung planks making a continuous platform. But that which is heaped upon the platform is hidden with muddy blankets.

The uniforms of the men—of various sorts, indicating that they are from many commands—are in shreds and spotted with stains of mould and earth; their heads are bound in cloths so that their faces are covered. The single drummer at the side of the column carries slung from his shoulder the shell of a drum. No flag flies from the staff at the column's head, but the staff is held erect.

Slowly the head of the line advances to the shadow of the wood, touches it and is swallowed. The leaders, the bare flag-staff, the drummer disappear; but still from the shade is heard the muffled rhythm of the drum. Still the column comes out of the mist, still it climbs the hill and passes with its endless articulated burden. At last, the rearmost couple disengages itself from the mist, ascends, and is swallowed by the shadow. There remain only the moonlight and the dusty hedgerow.

The question and an example answer are on the next page.

The extract you'll get in the exam will be longer than this.

How has the writer structured the text to interest you as a reader?

You could write about:

- what the writer focuses your attention on at the beginning of the source
- how and why the writer changes this focus as the source develops
- any other structural features that interest you

[8 marks]

The writer uses a cinematic writing style to structure the text, directing the reader's attention as the events unfold. Focusing the reader's attention in this way makes the reader feel as though they are a passive bystander to the mysterious events, and causes them to question whether they have witnessed something real or ghostly, which is unsettling.

At the beginning of the extract, the writer focuses the reader's attention on the surroundings. The scene includes "a pool of mist" and a "shadow of a wood" in the "moonlight". This dark and eerie setting acts as a narrative hook which making the reader feel unsettled, and creating a tense tone, which suggests that something strange or frightening might happen.

Gradually, the writer reveals a "monotonous rhythm" and a "strange shadowy column" moving from the mist. This increases the tension as the audience knows something is stirring in the darkness, but they don't know exactly what. This keeps the audience engaged and the suspense encourages them to read on to discover what will emerge from the darkness.

Eventually, the writer reveals that there are soldiers marching out of the shadows, but another mystery is introduced, as the soldiers are carrying something "hidden". This increases the anticipation as the audience want to know where the soldiers are going and what they are carrying. These questions are never answered, however, as the soldiers continue to march by, but they do not speak to each other. The lack of speech is unnerving, and makes the men feel almost ghostly, as they don't interact with their surroundings.

The extract ends by repeating some words from the opening paragraph, including, "mist", "shadow", "moonlight" and "dusty". This repetition suggests that the scene has returned to how it was before the men marched by, suggesting that they perhaps were never there at all, and the soldiers were ghosts or figments of someone's imagination. This realisation is shocking, and makes the reader feel unsettled.

This answer should be marked in accordance with the levels-based mark scheme on pages 73–74.

EXAMINATION PRACTICE

This extract is taken from a story called *The Interval*. In this passage, the main character, Mrs Wilton, visits an antique shop for a mysterious purpose.

Mrs. Wilton passed through a little alley leading from one of the gates which are around Regent's Park, and came out on the wide and quiet street. She walked along slowly, peering anxiously from side to side so as not to overlook the number. She pulled her furs closer round her; after her years in India this London damp seemed very harsh. A dense haze, grey and tinged ruddy, lay between the houses, sometimes blowing with a little wet kiss against the face. Mrs. Wilton's hair and eyelashes and her furs were powdered with tiny drops. But there was nothing in the weather to blur her sight; she could see the faces of people some distance off and read the signs on the shops.

Before the door of a dealer in antiques and second-hand furniture she paused and looked through the shabby uncleaned window at an unassorted heap of things, many of them of great value. She read the name fastened on the pane in white letters.

"Yes; this is the place."

She opened the door, which met her entrance with an ill-tempered jangle. From somewhere in the black depths of the shop the dealer came forward. He had a clammy white face, with a sparse black beard, and spectacles. Mrs. Wilton spoke to him in a low voice.

A look of complicity, of cunning, perhaps of irony, passed through the dealer's cynical and sad eyes. But he bowed gravely and respectfully.

"Yes, she is here, madam. Whether she will see you or not I do not know. She is not always well; she has her moods. And then, we have to be so careful. The police—Not that they would touch a lady like you. But..."

Mrs. Wilton followed him to the back of the shop, where there was a winding staircase. She knocked over a few things in her passage and stooped to pick them up, but the dealer kept muttering, "It does not matter—surely it does not matter." He lit a candle.

"You must go up these stairs. They are very dark; be careful. When you come to a door, open it and go straight in."

He stood at the foot of the stairs holding the light high above his head as she ascended.

1. How has the writer structured the text to interest you as a reader?

    You could write about:
    - what the writer focuses your attention on at the beginning of the source
    - how and why the writer changes this focus as the source develops
    - any other structural features that interest you   **[8 marks]**

QUESTION 4 – EXAM TECHNIQUE

This question tests how well you can evaluate the ideas and methods the writer has used in the text.

Example question

04   Focus this part of your answer on the second part of the source, **from line 28 to the end**.

A student said, "In this part of the story where Anita and Rosa get swept out to sea, I can't believe that Anita didn't react to the warning signs because the situation sounds really dangerous."

To what extent do you agree?

In your response, you could:
- consider Anita's reactions in this part of the story
- evaluate how the writer makes the situation dangerous
- support your response with references to the text   **[20 marks]**

In the exam, you'll get a full extract to answer the question. This is just a sample question to show you the question wording you can expect.

How to answer question 4

- This question covers AO4 (see **page xii** for a list of the AOs). It tests how well you can critically evaluate a text and give an opinion on how effective the writing is.
- The statement in the question will be made up of two parts. In the example above the two parts are: "Anita didn't react to the warning signs" and "the situation sounds really dangerous". To get top marks, you need to be able to respond to both parts of the statement.
- Make sure you only draw your answer from the lines specified in the question.
- You should write something to address each of the bullet points, and you need to provide evidence from the text to support your points.
- It's not enough to just spot techniques. You need to relate the techniques back to the statement in the question.
- This question is worth 20 marks. You should spend about 23 minutes on it.

Approaching the question

> This question is worth 20 marks, so you should jot down a quick plan before you start.

This question asks: "To what extent do you agree?" so you need to make a judgement. You should state your judgement at the start of your answer. Here are some suggested openings:

I strongly agree / disagree....	I somewhat agree / disagree...
I agree / disagree to an extent, however...	I agree that... but I disagree that....

The first bullet point may ask you to consider a character's reactions to something, or your own impressions of a character. You could include:

- what a character says, and how they say it.
- how a character is feeling.
- how they behave.
- whether their reaction is reasonable (or not), and why they might be acting in this way.

> Remember to consider any implied information too, for example, inferences and connotations (see **page 9**).

The second bullet point asks you to evaluate how effectively the writer has created a particular effect. You could think about:

- the **narrative viewpoint** the writer has used (**page 20**), e.g. have they used a first-person narrator to create a direct relationship with the reader, or an omniscient third-person narrator who knows what all the characters are thinking and feeling.
- the **words and phrases** the writer has used (**pages 8–9**), e.g. have they used **adjectives** to create a vivid image in the reader's mind or lots of **verbs** to create a sense of action.
- the language techniques the writer has used (**pages 11–12**), e.g. **similes**, **metaphors** or **personification** to make the text come alive for the reader.
- the sentences the writer has used (**pages 14–15**), e.g. have they used short sentences to create a fast **pace** and increase **tension**, or long sentences to slow the pace and create a calm **tone**.
- the structure the writer has used to reveal information (**pages 19–21**), e.g. have they used a **linear** or **non-linear structure**, have they used **flash-forwards** or **flashbacks** to hint at something and create tension.

> Make sure you back up your points with examples from the text and use PEEDL (**pages vi–vii**) to structure your answer.

This extract is taken from a short story by E. Nesbit.

A soft rain was falling. Umbrellas swayed and gleamed in the light of the streetlamps. The brightness of the shop windows reflected in the muddy mirror of the wet pavements. A miserable night, a dreary night, a night to tempt the wretched to the glimmering Embankment, and thence to the river, hardly wetter or cleaner than the gutters of the London streets. Yet the sight of these same streets was like lightning in the veins to a man who drove through them in a taxi piled with bags and suitcases. He leaned over the door of the taxi and looked eagerly, longingly, lovingly, at every sordid detail: the crowd on the pavement, its haste as intelligible to him as the rush of ants when their hill is disturbed by the spade; the glory and glow of corner pubs; the shifting dance of the gleaming wet umbrellas. It was England, it was London, it was home—and his heart swelled till he felt it in his throat. After ten years—the dream realised, the longing appeased.

A student, having read this extract, said, "In this part of the story, I can't believe the character is happy to be back, because London sounds miserable". To what extent do you agree?

In your response, you could:
- consider your own impressions of the scene
- evaluate how the writer conveys the character's reactions to the scene
- support your response with references to the text   **[20 marks]**

I disagree with the student's statement. Throughout the extract, the writer includes elements of the scene which could be considered miserable, for instance, the rain and the darkness, but describes them in a way that makes them seem beautiful. For example, the umbrellas are "gleaming" in the "soft" rain, and in the darkness, the shop windows emit a "brightness". The writer also uses literary techniques to make the "dreary night" seem more magical to the reader. The umbrellas are personified as doing a "shifting dance" which makes the city feel alive and jubilant. Romanticising the scene in this way helps to convey to the reader just how happy the character is to be back in London, as he can see beauty in the mundane surroundings.

As well as using imagery to describe the scene, the writer uses the character's actions and emotions to suggest how happy he is to be back. The character is described as leaning "over the door of the taxi", showing how desperate he is to witness "every sordid detail" despite the rain. This joy feels almost child-like in its eagerness, which helps the reader to easily understand his delight. This exhilaration is also reinforced when the writer says that seeing the streets "was like lightning in the veins" implying that energy and excitement is coursing through him. The triplet of the adverbs "eagerly, longingly, lovingly" reinforces the tone of sheer delight, and the mix of jubilant emotions that the character feels. The way that the writer presents the character's joy is infectious, and the reader too is swept up in the excitement of the homecoming.

This answer should be marked in accordance with the levels-based mark scheme on page 74.

This is just a sample extract and answer. In the exam, both the text and the answer will be longer.

EXAMINATION PRACTICE

This extract is from a short story called *Lonely Places* by Francis Buzzell. In it, a forty-year-old woman called Abbie Snover, lives with her servant, Chris in a town in America. She has been sent a dwarf orange tree all the way from China.

Under Abbie's constant attention, the little orange tree thrived. A tiny green orange appeared. Day by day she watched it grow, looking forward to the time when it would become large and yellow. The days grew shorter and colder, but she did not mind; every week the orange grew larger. After the first snow, she moved the tree into the downstairs bedroom. She placed it on a little stand in the South window. The inside blinds, which she had always kept as her mother liked them best—the lower blinds closed, the top blinds opened a little to let in the morning light—she now threw wide open so that the tree would get all of the sun. And she kept a fire in the small sheet-iron stove, for fear that the old, draughty wood furnace might not send up a steady enough heat through the register. When the nights became severe, she crept down the narrow, winding stairs, and through the cold, bare halls, to put an extra chunk of hardwood into the stove. Every morning she swept and dusted the room; the ashes and wood dirt around the stove gave her something extra to do near the orange tree.

"Abbie loves that orange tree more'n anything in the world," Chris cautioned the children when they came after cookies, "an' don't you dare touch it, even with your little finger."

The growing orange was as wonderful to the children as it was to Abbie. Instead of taking the cookies and hurrying home, they stood in front of the tree, their eyes round and big. And one day, when Abbie went to the laundry room to get the cookie-pail, Bruce Sanders snipped the orange from the tree.

The children were unnaturally still when Abbie came out of the laundry room. They did not rush forward to get the cookies. Abbie looked quickly at the tree; the pail of cookies dropped from her hands. She grabbed the two children nearest and shook them until their heads bumped together. Then she drove them all in front of her to the door and down the path to the gate, which she slammed shut behind them.

Once outside the gate the children ran, yelling: "Ab-bie Sno-ver, na—aa—ah! Ab-bie Sno-ver, na—aa—ah!"

Abbie, her hands trembling, her eyes hot, went back into the house. That was what came of letting them take fruit from the trees and vines in the yard; of giving them cookies every time they rang her doorbell. Well, there would be no more cookies, and Chris should be told never to let them come into the yard again.

1. A student, having read this extract, said, "The writer shows how much Abbie cares for the orange tree, so all our sympathy is with Abbie when the orange is cut from the tree."

    To what extent do you agree?

    In your response, you could:
    - consider Abbie's actions in the story
    - evaluate how the writer creates sympathy for Abbie
    - support your response with references to the text

    [20 marks]

QUESTION 5 – EXAM TECHNIQUE

This is the final question on paper 1. It's worth a whopping 40 marks.

Example question

05   Your school is asking students to contribute some creative writing for its website.

Either
Write a story about a risky journey as suggested by this picture.

Or
Describe a place you think is dangerous.

(24 marks for content and organisation
16 marks for technical accuracy)

[40 marks]

How to answer question 5

- This question covers AO5 and 6 (see **page xii** for a list of the AOs). It tests how well you can write clearly and imaginatively, and that you can suit your writing to different audiences and purposes. It also tests that you can structure your writing clearly, and that you can use different sentence structures and a wide vocabulary.

- This question also tests your spelling, punctuation and grammar. There are 16 marks available for technical accuracy (see **pages viii–xi**).

- You can pick either the image or the written prompt. You only need to respond to one task.

- The question will give you an audience and purpose. In the example above, you are writing a creative (i.e. entertaining) piece for other students at your school, so you need to make sure that your writing is appropriate.

- This question is worth 40 marks, and you should spend about 40–45 minutes on it. You should spend about 10 minutes on a plan, 25 minutes writing and 5-10 minutes checking and editing.

With the image prompt, you should include details beyond what is in the picture.

QUESTION 5 – WRITING A PLAN

It can be tempting to just start writing, especially when the clock is ticking, but a quick plan can make sure your writing is well structured and stays on track.

Planning

There's no right or wrong way to write a plan. You could use a spider diagram, a list or a table, just use whatever works best for you. Plans don't have to be in full sentences, so you can just jot down notes. Put a line through your plan if you don't want the examiner to look at it.

Things you could include in your plan:

 It can be helpful to develop a plot, characters and setting before the exam, then adapt your ideas to either the written or picture prompt in the exam.

Prompt

The question on the exam paper will give you either a written or picture prompt. You need to think about how this prompt can be incorporated into your story.

Characters

Decide who the main character is, and if there are any other characters. You could write down a couple of adjectives to describe their appearance and personality.

Setting

Choose where the story will take place, and whether it's happening in the past, present or future. The setting could shift, or it could all take place in the same location.

 You'll only have about 45 minutes to write your story, so don't make your plan too complicated with lots of characters and subplots.

Plot

Briefly jot down what will happen in the beginning, middle and end of your story. (See next page.)

Tone

Decide what kind of atmosphere you want to create, e.g. light-hearted and humorous, unsettling and tense.

When you're writing your plan, you might want to think about what perspective you're going to tell your story from (**page 20**) what tense you want to write in (**page 8**) and what sort of structural features you want to include (**page 19–21**).

 Don't copy plots or characters from books, films or computer games. The examiner will recognise that the ideas aren't your own, and will reduce your marks accordingly.

QUESTION 5 – WRITING STORIES

Good stories need a beginning, middle and end that will keep the reader's attention until the very last word.

Writing stories

Try to include some ambitious vocabulary in your writing. You're more likely to be awarded marks for being adventurous than for playing it safe. Don't go overboard though!

Sometimes you might be asked to write a story, other times you might be asked to write the opening or ending to a story. Read the question carefully so you know what you need to do.

If you write a story, you should include a beginning, middle and end. Make sure you use your time well. Don't spend too long on the opening, only to run out of time and not write an ending.

Beginning

Start your story with a narrative hook, i.e. something interesting or exciting.

You could use **foreshadowing** to hint at something exciting.	Of course, I didn't know it when I woke up, but today would change the course of my life forever.
You could start in the middle of the action to create tension.	I was screaming until my lungs were burning and my throat was raw, but no one was coming to help.

Middle

This is where you develop your plot and characters. Remember to use different linguistic techniques (see **pages 11–12**) to make your descriptions vivid, and structural techniques to make your writing interesting for the reader (**pages 19–21**).

End

Even if you're running out of time, make sure you write an ending to your story, but avoid clichés like "it was all a dream" and "they lived happily ever after".

You could write an ending which brings the action to a satisfying conclusion.	After that day, I never went on a risky journey again.
You could leave the reader with an unanswered question or a **plot twist**.	After all these years, I had been certain that the cursed locket had been destroyed in the fire, but yesterday, a small jewellery box arrived in the post. I haven't dared open it.

QUESTION 5 – WRITING DESCRIPTIONS

Unlike stories, descriptions don't need a plot. Instead, they're a piece of writing that give a detailed image of a person, place or object.

Descriptions

Even though they don't have a plot, you should still plan a description to make sure you have enough to write about and you've thought carefully about what you want to include, and the order you want to reveal information to the reader.

Use literary techniques to add interest to your descriptions. Have a look back at **page 11–12** if you need a reminder.

Good descriptions show the reader something, rather than tell them something. That means including inferences and implicit information.

Describing a place

In the exam, you might be given a picture prompt or a written prompt. The prompt will provide a starting point for your description, but it will usually allow for lots of different interpretations, so you can use your imagination and be creative.

There are no right or wrong ways to interpret the prompt. You will be assessed on how well you can write creatively, and that you can structure your writing clearly, and use correct spelling, punctuation and grammar.

Here are some ideas you could include in a description of a place:

- What country is the place in? It could be somewhere real, or somewhere you've made up.

- What time of day is it?

- What season is it, and what's the weather like?

- Is it somewhere urban (in a town or city) or somewhere rural (in the countryside)?

- What can you see? Are there any buildings, people, animals, plants, mountains etc?

- If you're describing buildings, what are they made from? Are the buildings new or old? Are they well cared for or have they fallen into disrepair?

- How would you describe the atmosphere of the place? Is it calm and peaceful, dangerous and scary?

Describing a person

Here are some prompts to help you describe a character. You don't have to include all of them in your description, and there's plenty more features you could include.

- When is the description set? Is it in the past, the present or the future?

- Are they male, female or non-binary?

- Are they old, young or somewhere in between?

- Are they tall, short or average height?

- Do they have a slim build or are they stocky or muscular?

- What is their ethnicity?

- What colour are their eyes? What colour hair do they have? Is it long, short, curly or straight?

- What are they wearing? What does that tell you about them? i.e. if they're wearing scrubs, it might tell you they work in a hospital.

- What kind of person are they, and how might you show that? i.e. a kind person might have crinkles round their eyes from smiling a lot.

- What mood are they in? i.e. an anxious person might be chewing their nails.

These two passages describe the same character. The first description is very basic and simply tells the reader facts about the character. The second passage uses linguistic techniques to describe the character, and suggests information to the reader, rather than telling them outright.

> Lucy Judd was quite vain. She was about 19, with pale skin and wore a lot of makeup. She had green eyes and red hair that she wore in a bun. She had just broken up with her boyfriend, Jackson, and was waiting for him to call her.

Lucy Judd stared at herself in the mirror, She turned her face this way, then that, stretching her porcelain skin. Was that a wrinkle? Surely, not. She wasn't even 20 yet. She sighed and reached for her eyeliner from the assortment of bottles, tubes and powders on her dressing table. She drew a black line across the top lid, and carefully smudged it with her finger. Jackson had told her once that the kohl made her eyes sparkle like emeralds, so she had worn eyeliner every day after that. She picked up a brush and began raking angrily through her auburn hair as she thought of him. Realising she had brushed the same spot half a dozen times, she set the brush down and twisted the copper rope into a bun and secured it. She glanced down at her phone, willing it to light up.

This implies Lucy is vain because she's looking at herself closely in the mirror. She cares about her appearance.

This figurative language suggests Lucy has pale skin.

Lucy has a lot of products on her dressing table. This implies that she puts a lot of effort into how she looks.

This simile tells the reader that Lucy has green eyes.

This suggests that Lucy cares a lot about what Jackson thinks. He must be important to her, but she's also angry at him.

A metaphor makes the description of Lucy's hair more interesting. Describing it as a 'rope' suggests it's long.

This suggests she's desperate for a call or message on her phone.

An online competition for story writing is being held, and you have decided to enter.

Write a story with the title 'Luck'.

(24 marks for content and organisation and
16 marks for technical accuracy)

[40 marks]

Plan:

Luck: can be good or bad. Story where good and bad luck mix, and where bad luck can turn to good.

Beginning: Olive (older lady in her 70s) is having a lucky morning. She is making porridge when the phone rings to say her entry into a photo competition has won a voucher.

Middle: On her way into town, she speaks to her next-door neighbours, the Richardsons, who've had an unlucky morning, their flight was cancelled so have missed out on a holiday.

End: Mr Richardson phones Olive to tell her that her house is on fire, but he was able to phone the fire station early and damage was minimal. Lucky that the Richardsons were at home.

Symbols of bad luck: number 13, black cats, broken mirrors, crossing under ladders

Luck

Olive Caruthers was very content, thank you very much. She lived alone in a lovely little detached bungalow (number 13), in a lovely little cul-de-sac with lovely little neighbours. Despite being a senior citizen, Olive lived her life to the fullest, and nothing could slow her down (especially now she had an off-peak OAP bus pass). She had been up since 8 o'clock sharp, as she did every morning, and was making her usual breakfast — hot, milky porridge on the stove, studded with prunes and a spoonful of strawberry jam. As she stirred the pan, her phone began to ring.

"Nine-oh-three-two-eight!" she trilled, brushing some wayward oats off her apron.

"Hello, please may I speak to Mrs. Caruthers?"

"Speaking."

"Oh, hello, Mrs Caruthers. It's Gordon Haltwhistle from the Swindonbourne Photography Society. We're delighted to inform you that you've won our portrait competition, and we have a pair of restaurant vouchers for you. We'd love you to pop by so the local press can take a picture with your winning entry."

Olive beamed. She just knew her photo was special. Of course, she had hoped that it would win something, but first prize! What luck!

"I'll come right away!" Olive exclaimed as she replaced the receiver.

A mere 6 and a half minutes later, Olive had donned her smartest coat, fastened her best silver broach to the lapel and picked up her handbag. She was just locking the front door when she saw the Richardson's car pull up next door.

"Funny," thought Olive, "I could have sworn they'd left for Tenerife this morning." She wandered over to the car, excited to tell Penny Richardson that her photo had won first prize.

"Penny, dear!" she hollered flapping her hand in greeting, but she stopped in her tracks as she saw Mr Richardson's face as he swung out of the drivers' seat. "Is everything alright, Mike?"

Mike shook his head and opened the boot, revealing three suitcases. "Baggage handling strike at the airport, so our flight got cancelled." He grimaced as he heaved an enormous hard-shell case on to the pavement.

"Oh no!" cried Olive. "What terrible luck. I'm so sorry." Mike shrugged, and helped seven-year-old Penny out of the passenger side, whose headphones were firmly stuck in her ears, and whose button nose was a mere inch from the screen of the tablet she was holding.

"It's annoying, but it's not the end of the world. The airline said they'd put us on standby." The Richardson's black cat, Milo, strolled out from the hedge and crossed in front of them. Miaowing contentedly and slinking through Mike's legs.

"Well, at least someone's happy you're home." She smiled, deciding not to tell the Richardsons about her triumph at the photography competition. It wasn't becoming to boast, especially when they'd had such rotten luck.

Olive bid them farewell and walked to the end of the cul-de-sac and waited for the number 83 bus. One should be along shortly. She glanced at her wristwatch.

Olive had taken the bus right through to the centre of town. She'd popped into The Broken Mirror, her favourite coffee shop, for a strong cup of tea and a slice of their thick, nutty flapjack (she felt very hungry, and couldn't work out why). She then pottered along the High Street. There had been quite a lot of building work going on near the Theatre Royale, and she'd had to duck under a couple of ladders on her way to the Swindonbourne Photography Society.

Just as she was about to cross the street, she heard a buzzing sound coming from her handbag. It was that silly mobile phone her son had insisted that she carry everywhere. She fished it out of her bag and poked roughly at the big green button.

"Hello, Olive Caruthers speaking."

"Olive! It's Mike! From next-door. The fire crew are here. It's your house. I think there's minimal damage. But..."

"What!" Olive exclaimed, shakily. "A fire? Where?"

"Your kitchen. You left the porridge on the hob."

This answer should be marked in accordance with the levels-based mark schemes on pages 75–77.

EXAMINATION PRACTICE

A magazine has asked for contributions for their creative writing section.

Either

1. Write a description suggested by this picture.

or

2. Write a story about a place which has been abandoned.

(24 marks for content and organisation
16 marks for technical accuracy)
[40 marks]

PAPER 2
Writers' viewpoints and perspectives

Information about Paper 2

Written exam: 1 hour 45 minutes
80 marks
Q1–5 are compulsory
50% of the qualification grade

Specification coverage

Section A will test AO1, AO2 and AO3
Section B will test AO5 and AO6

Questions

One multiple-choice question, two longer form
questions and two extended-writing questions.

EXAM TEXTS

You will be given two sources to accompany Paper 2. You'll need to use these sources to answer all the questions in Section A.

What to expect from Sources A and B

You should read the questions, and then read the sources. You should spend about 15 minutes on this.

The sources will be printed in a separate booklet so they're easier to refer to.

Text type

Both sources will be literary non-fiction (based on real events). One will be written in the 20th or 21st century (1900–to present day), the other will be written in the 19th century (1800s). 19th-century texts can sound different to modern texts (have a look at **pages 39–40**).

Literary non-fiction tends to be written in a more descriptive way than other non-fiction texts and may use similar linguistic techniques to fiction texts (see **pages 11–12**).

Word count

Each source will be around 600–700 words.

Introduction

There will be a couple of sentences at the start of each extract which will briefly introduce the **author**, the **publication date** and **context**.

Glossary

A couple of difficult words might be defined at the end of the text, but don't rely on this.

Topic

Both texts will be about a similar topic, but their authors might have different **viewpoints** and **perspectives**.

Form

The texts could be any **form** of non-fiction writing, for example, an autobiography, a letter, a diary or a newspaper article.

Purpose

The **purpose** will depend on the form and intended audience, and there may be more than one purpose, for example, the purpose of an autobiography might be to **inform** and to **entertain** the reader.

Line numbers

The line numbers down the left-hand side of the page can be used to navigate the text. Some of the questions will use line numbers to specify which part of the text you need to draw your answer from, and you will only be expected to draw your answer from that part of the text.

19TH-CENTURY TEXTS

Texts from the 1800s will often sound different to more modern texts, and you might be less familiar with the text's context.

19th-century texts — writing style

Language

Older texts often sound more **formal** than modern texts. This is partly because they use language which is more complicated and sophisticated. 19th-century writers often chose longer words over shorter ones, for example, 'desire', 'declare' or 'earnest' instead of 'want', 'say' or 'keen'.

Texts from the 1800s might use words and phrases that aren't common today, e.g. 'governess' (female tutor), 'looking-glass' (mirror), 'beastly' (horrible).

19th-century texts, particularly letters, tend to use **superlatives** (adjectives with 'most' or ending '-est') such as 'most beautiful', 'most charming, 'dearest' and 'kindest'. They also might use **intensifiers** (a word that goes before an adjective to emphasise it), such as 'very', 'truly', 'dear'. Writers often used superlatives and intensifiers to flatter the reader, as flattery was considered polite.

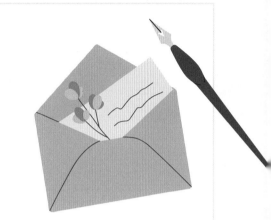

Unfamiliar words will probably be defined for you in the exam.

Sentence structure

Texts written in the 1800s also tend to use longer, more complex sentence structures with multiple **clauses**. Sometimes they might use **inversion** or a less common word order which might not be as easy for modern readers to follow. Compare this example written in the 19th century, to the version below which has been rewritten in more modern English.

> It gives me great satisfaction to hear that you are enjoying the sea air and like the place which you now occupy. I wish I could pay your Mamma a visit there and see you again, my dear little niece, for I long to have that pleasure, and must resign myself at being deprived of it some time longer.

> I'm pleased that you are enjoying the sea air and that you like the place you're living in. I would like to visit your mother and see you again, my dear little niece, and although I am very keen to see you both, I've got to wait a little bit longer.

19th-century texts — context

Context refers to historical events and social attitudes when a text was written. It's helpful to understand the context of 19th-century texts so you know what was expected at that time.

Society and family life

Social classes were more defined in the 19th century. There was a very clear structure of upper, middle and lower classes. The wealthy were very rich, and the poor lived in poverty.

Attitudes towards men and women were very different. Women were often expected to behave in a certain way, especially upper-class women. For example, they were expected to be accomplished (able to sing, play musical instruments, paint and speak a foreign language), as well as behave politely and modestly. Women were also seen as weaker and less intelligent than men, who were supposed to protect and provide for their wives.

Women from all social classes were often in charge of their household, although wealthy women would have had servants to help run the house and care for children. Wealthy women didn't work, whereas poorer women may have needed a job to help contribute to the family's income.

Education

Children from wealthier families may have been educated at home by a private tutor or governess, whereas children from poorer families usually received very little education and would have been expected to get a job from a young age, such as cleaning chimneys, selling flowers or working in a factory.

Hobbies and travel

Most poor people were illiterate, so reading was mainly a pastime for the rich. Many texts from this period would be aimed at a wealthier readership.

Overseas travel was very uncommon, so reading a piece of travel writing might be the only way a person could experience what life was like abroad, as there was no Internet and little photography. This meant a writer would have to describe their experiences clearly because they would be so unfamiliar.

Wealthier families in the 1800s might travel around Britain, but they would use horse-drawn carriages, so journeys were slow and uncomfortable. Later in the century, steam trains made travel quicker and smoother.

These are just a few examples of how life in the 19th century was different to today. In the exam, if you need to comment on context, think about any notable differences or similarities you can draw from the texts.

AUDIENCE

Non-fiction authors adapt their writing so it's suitable for their audience.

Audience

Some non-fiction texts try to appeal to lots of different readers, whereas others will be more specific.

Age

- A text explaining how to get online aimed at older people might use simple, clear language because the readers might be unfamiliar with using the Internet.
- An article about learning to drive might use informal, chatty language or **slang** to appeal to teenage readers.

Gender

- A 19th-century text giving advice on successful marriages might use **direct address** aimed at women, because wives were expected to keep their husbands happy.

Wealth and status

- A piece of travel writing might use lots of **superlative adjectives** to describe a luxury hotel to appeal to wealthy readers.

Opinions and interests

- An article about mountain biking might use lots of technical language or **jargon** (specialist terms) to appeal to readers who already know a lot about mountain biking.
- A text about bad behaviour in toddlers might try to create a **sympathetic tone** to appeal to parents experiencing the same issues.

These are just a few examples of different audiences. There are many more.

One of the texts will be from the 19th century, so the writers' attitudes may be influenced by the context of the 1800s. Look at **page 40** for more information.

PURPOSE

Before you start analysing the texts, it's helpful to narrow down their **purpose**, i.e. why they were written.

Purpose

Inform / Explain

Texts that inform or explain tell the reader information, usually something they don't already know. For example, a history book about the Roman Empire or a newspaper article about an earthquake abroad. They might include **facts** and **statistics** to make their writing seem more reliable and might use an **objective writing style** (see **page 55**) to appear more authoritative.

Entertain

Texts that entertain are written for the audience's enjoyment. For example, an autobiography is designed to interest the reader. Entertaining texts might use **figurative** language and vivid descriptions to make the text come alive for the reader (see **pages 11–12**).

Argue

Texts that argue state the writer's opinion, and try to encourage the audience to agree with them or change their own opinion. These texts might use **rhetorical devices** or **bias** (see **page 55**) to try to convince the reader.

Advise

Texts that advise help the reader to do something. For example, an article about creating a household budget or how to eat healthily. They might use clear language and **simple sentences** to make the text easy for the reader to follow and understand.

Persuade

Persuasive texts want the reader to do something. For example, a letter persuading a reader to donate money to charity. Persuasive texts often appeal to the reader's emotions, and they might use **direct address** and **emotive language**.

Texts that argue and texts that persuade often share some similarities, but texts that argue are often more forceful, whereas persuasive texts tend to be gentler, and play on the reader's emotions.

Instruct

Texts that instruct tell the reader how to do things, for example a recipe or a set of instructions for building furniture. They often use short, clear sentences that use **imperative verbs**. Texts are usually structured into a numbered list, and each sentence has to be read in a particular order.

Most texts have multiple purposes. For example, a leaflet about a theme park might inform the reader about ticket prices and opening hours, but it might also try to persuade the reader to visit the theme park with descriptions that make it sound exciting.

QUESTION 1 – EXAM TECHNIQUE

The first question in the exam tests your ability to spot information.

Example question

01 Read again the first part of **Source A**, from **lines 1 to 5**.

Choose four statements below which are **true**. [4 marks]

In the exam, you'll get a full extract to answer the question. This is just a sample question to show you the question wording you can expect.

How to answer question 1

- This question tests the first part of AO1. (See **page xii** for the AOs.) You have to pick out information from a text. The information might be explicit (clearly stated in the text), or you might have to make an inference.

- The question is multiple choice. You will be given eight statements about the extract. Four statements will be true, and four will be false. You need to identify the true (or false) statements.

- You should shade a box next to the statements to show which ones you have chosen. If you tick the box you risk losing marks.

- Make sure you take your answers from the part of the text specified by the line numbers. If you take your answer from any other part of the source, you won't get the mark.

- Only select four statements. If you choose any more than four, you will have marks deducted.

- You will get one mark per correct answer.

- You should spend about 4 minutes on this question.

Correcting question 1

If you change your mind about an answer to question 1, cross out the whole box. If you change your mind again and want to select a statement that has been crossed out, then draw a circle around the box.

A	The writer has never ridden a horse.	○
B	The writer is afraid of horses.	
C	Most people at the ranch ride horses daily.	○

AQA GCSE **English Language – Paper 2**   43

This extract from a letter was written by Elinore Pruitt Stewart in 1878. In it, she describes camping in the desert.

1.   After we left the canyon, I saw the most beautiful sight. It seemed as if we were driving through a golden haze. The violet shadows were creeping up between the hills, while behind us the snow-capped peaks were catching the sun's last rays. On every side of us stretched the poor, hopeless desert, the sage, grim and determined to live in spite of starvation, and the great, bare,
5.   desolate buttes*. The beautiful colours turned to amber and rose, and then to the general tone, dull grey. Then we stopped to camp, and such a scurrying around to gather brush for the fire and to get supper. Everything tasted so good! Then we raised the wagon tongue and spread the wagon sheet over it and made a camp. We made our beds on the warm, soft sand and went to bed. It was too beautiful a night to sleep, so I put my head out to look and to think.
10.   I saw a coyote come trotting along and I felt sorry for him, having to hunt food in so barren a place, but when presently I heard the whirr of wings and I felt sorry for the chicken he had seized.

buttes — columns of rock

Read the extract from lines **1 to 12**.

Choose four statements below which are **true**.   **[4 marks]**

  A The writer describes the sun setting.   ☐

  B There is snow high in the mountains.   ☐

  C The desert is very hot.   ☐

  D The campers sleep on the sand.   ☐

  E The campers collect firewood.   ☐

  F The writer dislikes camping.   ☐

  G The writer was scared by the coyote.   ☐

  H The coyote fails to catch a chicken.   ☐

A, B, D, E

⭐ This example asks you to look at the first 12 lines. In the exam, you may be asked to look at a shorter extract.

EXAMINATION PRACTICE

> This extract is by an American traveller called Nellie Bly. She describes arriving at a hotel in Mexico City.
>
> 1.   We soon arrived at the Hotel Yturbide, and were assigned rooms by the affable clerk. The lowest floor in Mexico is the cheapest. The higher up one goes the higher they find the price. The reason of this is that at the top one escapes any possible dampness, and can get the light and sun.
> 5.   Our room had a red brick floor. It was large, but had no ventilation except the glass doors which opened onto the balcony. There was a little iron bed in each corner of the room, a table, washstand, and wardrobe.

1.   Read the extract from lines **1 to 7**.

     Choose four statements below which are **true**.   **[4 marks]**

     A   The clerk was friendly.   ☐
     B   The rooms on the top floor are the cheapest.   ☐
     C   The rooms on the top floor of the hotel are less likely to be damp. ☐
     D   Nellie's hotel room had a tiled floor.   ☐
     E   Nellie's hotel room is small.   ☐
     F   The glass doors in Nellie's room provided the only ventilation.   ☐
     G   Nellie's room had a balcony.   ☐
     H   Nellie's room had one bed.   ☐

QUESTION 2 – EXAM TECHNIQUE

This question asks you to look at both sources and summarise similarities or differences.

Example question

02 You need to refer to **Source A** and **Source B** for this question.

Both sources describe how the dolphins behave.

Use details from **both** sources to write a summary of what you understand about the similar behaviour of the dolphins. **[8 marks]**

> In the exam, you'll get a full extract to answer the question. This is just a sample question to show you the question wording you can expect.

How to answer question 2

- This question tests AO1. You need to find and understand information from two texts, and combine evidence to answer the question. (See **xii** for the AOs.)
- You will have to look at the two sources and summarise either similarities or differences.
- The information might be clearly stated, or it might be implied. You should look out for both.
- You need to look at both sources in a similar amount of detail.
- This question is worth 8 marks. You should spend about 8–9 minutes on it.
- Linking words can help to show the examiner that you're looking at both the sources. For some examples of linking works, have a look at **page vii**.

Worked example

To answer this question well, you should use **SQI** to structure your response: statement, quotation, inference. Have a look at the example below.

These are just short example extracts. The texts you'll get in the exam will be much longer.

Source A is taken from the foreword of a cookbook published in 2018.

To just see food as something purely nutritional is to ignore its most magical property. Simply put, food brings people together. And the most wondrous thing? This magic can be unlocked by anyone — you're never too old nor too young to learn how to cook.

Source B is from a book, *Science in the Kitchen*, published in 1892.

There is no department of life where superior intelligence is more needed than in the selection and preparation of food, upon which so largely depend the health and physical welfare of the family circle.

---

02 Use details from **both** sources to write a summary of what you understand about the differences about cooking.

---

1. Statement: Find a similarity or difference

The author of Source A thinks anyone can learn how to cook, whereas the author of Source B suggests that only intelligent people should learn to cook.

2. Quotation: Use a short quote to support your point

Source A — The magic of cooking "can be unlocked by anyone".

Source B — "There is no department of life where superior intelligence is more needed".

Often, writers will show you something rather than tell you something outright. You need to be able to spot these clues, so you can make an inference about the author's meaning.

3. Inference: Suggest why the authors might have a similar or different opinion

The author of Source B believes that the "physical welfare" of the family depends on the "preparation of food". Since the author of Source B thinks food is so important to the health of their family, they only trust someone intelligent to prepare food. The author may have this opinion because medicine and healthcare were less advanced in the 19th century, and people had to be careful to look after their health, including their diet. On the other hand, the author of Source A thinks food is more than "purely nutritional" suggesting that they see food as something pleasurable. As a result, they are more relaxed about who prepares food.

Source A is from an article from 2012 about rescuing animals from the illegal pet trade.

Sammy is a three-year-old capuchin monkey who was illegally brought into the UK. He had been kept alone in a cramped cage in a shed, which had not been adequately cleaned in some time, and he had no access to natural light. When we rescued him, we observed all the behaviours of domestication. He showed no fear of human interaction, and when we approached the cage, he made several attempts to communicate, indicating he wanted to be fed. He had no reservations about climbing on to me when I opened his cage. Although he was not underweight, we did observe some bald spots, predominately on his tail, likely a sign of over-grooming, behaviour typically seen in captive primates. Sammy was taken to a nearby monkey sanctuary, and, after observation, was eventually placed in an enclosure with other capuchin monkeys. He initially showed bullying behaviour, not uncommon in rescued animals, but, with time, we are hopeful that this will improve.

Source B is from *Apes and Monkeys* by R L Gardener.

During the winter of 1891 there lived in Central Park, New York, five little brown monkeys, all of the same kind and occupying the same cage. One of the most cunning and happiest of all little monkeys was in this group, and his name was Mickie. He was not very talkative except when he wished for food or drink. Whenever I entered the cage Mickie perched himself above the door to surprise me by jumping on my neck. He then affectionately threw his arms around my neck and licked my cheeks, and chattered in his sweet, plaintive tones. Mickie did not belong to the park. He was only kept as a guest of the city during the absence of his master in Europe. He had a genuine sense of humour and sometimes played pranks upon the others, very much to their annoyance. On one occasion Mickie got the tail of another monkey around one of the bars of the cage. He sat down and held it while its owner screamed with rage and scuffled to get away. During this time Mickie's face wore a broad, satanic grin, and he did not release it until he had tired of the fun.

You need to refer to **Source A** and **Source B** for this question. Both sources describe the behaviour of monkeys.

Use details from **both** sources to write a summary of what you understand about the similar behaviour of monkeys.   **[8 marks]**

Both Sources describe the behaviour of wild monkeys that have been taken from their native countries to be kept as pets, Sammy in the UK and Mickie in America. As a result of their domestication, neither monkey is afraid of humans. Sammy climbs on to his rescuer and Mickie jumps on the writer's neck. Part of their confident behaviour towards humans might be because they know that humans provide food. Sammy indicates "he wanted to be fed" and Mickie wasn't talkative unless "he wished for food". This shows that both monkeys interact confidently with humans because they know that if they approach humans, they are likely to be rewarded with food.

Both Sammy and Mickie show aggressive behaviour towards other monkeys. This may be because they are both used to living without company. Sammy had been "kept alone" until he went to the sanctuary and Mickie was only "a guest of the city" because his master was "in Europe". This suggests that neither Sammy nor Mickie are used to socialising with other primates. Sammy exhibits "bullying behaviour" and Mickie plays "pranks" which are very aggressive, causing the other monkeys to scream "with rage". This suggests that both monkeys have behavioural problems since they have been taken from the wild.

EXAMINATION PRACTICE

Source A is taken from an online newspaper. The writer gives a review of a Christmas market from 2019.

It never ceases to amaze me just how busy these markets get: thousands upon thousands descend in pursuit of a bratwurst, a cup of mulled wine and a sprinkling of Christmas magic. As I survey the cutesy little wooden huts, I spy all the usual suspects: vast pyramids of delicious fudge; charming wooden toys, that may (or may not) have been massed-produced in China; and of course, a rainbow assortment of pick 'n' mix with an eye-watering mark-up. This heady mix of sights, sounds and scents creates the perfect trap for families with young children. Rosy-cheeked youngsters tug on their parents' sleeves for toys, sweets, and a two-minute ride on the enormous, gilded carousel. After the carousel, (if you're not feeling too queasy) there's fresh sugar doughnuts, steaming mugs of hot chocolate and a penny arcade filled with bright lights and music that will leave your wallet much lighter than when you entered.

Source B was written by Isabella Bird, in 1869. Here she describes a night market in Edinburgh.

The High Street is filled with a densely compacted, loitering, brawling, buying, selling, singing, cursing, quarrelsome crowd—a nocturnal market vigorously proceeds under difficulties—men and women puff their wares with powerful tones and coarse wit—wheelbarrows with flaring lights, from which the poorest of the poor are buying the unwholesome refuse of the shops, stale fish, and stale vegetables—boys vending laces, nuts, whistles—women hawking tin and crockery ware, all eager, pushing, poor. Add to these, the exhibitors of penny-shows and penny cheats, the singers of vulgar and improper songs, the vendors of popular melodies and penny narrations of crime, and an idea may be formed of the noisy traffic of the High Street.

1. You need to refer to **Source A** and **Source B** for this question.

   Both sources describe a local market.

   Use details from **both** sources to write a summary of what you understand about the differences between the markets.

   [8 marks]

QUESTION 3 – EXAM TECHNIQUE

This question asks you to refer to just one source, and to explain how a writer uses language.

Example question

03 You now need to refer only to **Source A** from **lines 24 to 36**.

How does the writer use language to describe the garden? **[12 marks]**

In the exam, you'll get a full extract to answer the question. This is just a sample question to show you the question wording you can expect.

How to answer question 3

- This question covers the language part of AO2. (See **page xii** for the AOs.) It tests how well you can understand **implicit information**, i.e. information that is not directly stated in the text.

- You only need to look at one of the sources and select information from the line numbers specified in the question.

- You need to focus your answer on the thing specified in the question. In the example above, only answers that mention the garden will be awarded marks.

- It's not enough to just spot techniques. You need to write about how the writer uses language and the effect that it has on the reader.

- This question is worth 12 marks. You should spend about 14 minutes on it.

- This question is very similar to the language part of question 2 on Paper 1. To remind yourself of how to answer this question, turn to **pages 8–9 and 11–12**.

You'll need to use PEEDL to structure your answer. **See pages vi–vii for** more on using PEEDL.

Source A is a description of the town of Nome, Alaska, by a traveller, Mary Kellogg Sullivan.

How easily the long and graceful breakers rolled and broke upon the sands. With what music the foam-tipped wavelets spread their edges, like the lace-trimmed ruffles on some lady's gown, upon the smooth and glistening beach. How the white tents everywhere looked like doves of peace just alighted, and the little boats danced up and down on the river. I was glad to be there. I enjoyed it. Nothing, not even the hard work, the storms, nor the bitter Arctic winter which came afterwards ever erased from my memory the beautiful pictures of river, sea and sky repeatedly displayed during those first novel and busy days at Nome.

You now need to refer only to **Source A**.

How does the writer use language to describe the scene?   **[12 marks]**

The writer uses positive imagery to describe the scene. She uses the simile, "like the lace-trimmed ruffles on some lady's gown" to describe the foamy waves hitting the beach. The image of "lace-trimmed ruffles" suggests that the foam is beautiful and delicate, and creates a clear picture in the reader's mind of the bubbles in the foam by comparing it to lace. The author also describes the sound of the waves as being like "music". This sensory language helps the reader to imagine the melodic sounds of the water, and immerses the reader in the scene by describing both what they can hear as well as see.

The writer continues this positive imagery by using the simile "like doves of peace" to describe the crests of the waves. This suggests that the waves are tipped with white foam and helps the reader imagine the movement of the water, by comparing it to a flock of white birds taking flight. This suggests the waves are graceful and beautiful, just like doves. The writer continues this jubilant tone by using personification to describe the boats dancing on the river, implying that the boats are happy and joyful, which contributes to the positive mood of the scene.

The writer juxtaposes the peaceful, beautiful scene with a flashforward when she recalls "the storms" and the "bitter Arctic winter which came afterwards", suggesting that there are difficulties ahead. This makes the scene seem even more magical because we know that it is fleeting.

This answer should be marked in accordance with the levels-based mark scheme on page 78.

This is just a short example extract. The extract and response you'll give in the exam will be longer.

EXAMINATION PRACTICE

This extract is from the book *Oxford Mountaineering Essays* published in 1912. The author describes a mountain range in France.

I remember one evening sitting above the Col de Vosa and watching the glow of the sunset on Mont Blanc. The entire range of peaks from the Dôme du Goûter to the Aiguille Verte blazed with colour down to a point a little above where the ragged fringe of the moraines* slide into the grassy upland. There a hard line of shadow reflected the contour of the hill on which I sat. As the sun sank, this line of shadow crept up the mountainside with almost visible speed, till only the topmost pinnacles kept their colour, like a row of beacon-lights flaming above the darkened valley. Gradually they in their turn paled and died.

But it is when most onlookers turn away, that the mountains begin to live. When the fire has left the snow, when the rock ridges leap out cold and black, when the fissures of the ice cliffs yawn pitilessly once again, the real character of the place is shown. The mountains are cruel and angry. Traffic with them is not friendship, but war. All the mountaineer's thrill of conquest is the thrill of victory over an enemy, but whose resources are endless and whose ally is the storm. Snow mountains are seldom friendly. Sometimes they seem to smile, but their welcome, for all its glitter, is treacherous and cruel.

moraines — patches of soil, rock and debris

1. In the extract above, how does the writer use language to describe the mountains? **[12 marks]**

QUESTION 4 – EXAM TECHNIQUE

This question asks you to compare Source A and Source B. This time you need to think about the writers' attitudes.

Example question

04 For this question, you need to refer to the **whole of Source A**, together with the **whole of Source B**.

Compare how the writers convey their different attitudes to the journey.

In your answer, you could:
- compare their different attitudes to travelling
- compare the methods the writers use to convey their attitudes
- support your answer with references to both texts **[16 marks]**

In the exam, you'll get a full extract to answer the question. This is just a sample question to show you the question wording you can expect.

How to answer question 4

- This question tests AO3. (See **page xii** for the AOs.) You need to identify writers' ideas and attitudes, and compare the methods used.
- You need to include quotes and examples from both sources.
- Make sure you've responded to each of the bullet points in the question.
- You need to focus your answer on the thing specified in the question. In the example above, only answers that mention the journey will be awarded marks.
- To get the very best marks, you need to compare the two sources. You need to find similar elements between the two texts and comment on how their attitudes differ.
- This question is worth 16 marks. You should spend about 18 minutes on it.

You'll need to use PEEDL to structure your answer. **See pages vi–vii for more** on using PEEDL.

QUESTION 4 – WRITERS' ATTITUDES

A writer's attitude is what they think about a certain topic. Sometimes their attitude is obvious, but sometimes it might only be implied. Analysing linguistic features can help you to work out how they feel.

Writers' techniques

Tone

Tone is the feeling that a writer is trying to create. In non-fiction texts, a writer might use a **personal tone** to try to establish a friendly relationship with the reader. A writer might achieve this using **direct address** by using the pronoun 'you' to talk directly to the reader.

"Guys, you've got to buy a ticket before you get on the train."

Texts with an **impersonal tone** don't try to create a relationship with the reader, instead they sound more distant and formal. Writers can create an impersonal tone by avoiding direct address and by using the **passive voice** (see **page 15**).

Tickets must be purchased before travelling.

Style

Style includes the writer's choice of language, sentence forms and structure. For example, newspaper articles will often follow a recognisable style. They are often written in the **third person** and are in the **past tense**.

The Prime Minster has visited a local hospital today following reports that he is down in the opinion polls.

Register

Register is the language used to suit a specific purpose. If you're writing to someone you know, you might create an **informal register** by using chatty or **colloquial** (casual) **language**.

"Hiya mate. How's it going?"

If you're writing to someone you don't know, you might use a **formal register** and **Standard English** (see **page x**)

Dear Sir,
I hope this letter finds you well.

A writer's attitude might also be linked to the text's purpose. Turn to **page 42** for more on purpose.

Biased writing

Bias is when an author gives an unbalanced opinion, usually with the intention of trying to convince the reader to agree with them. Signs of biased writing might include:

Hyperbole is when something has been over-exaggerated to make it sound a lot better (or worse) than it is.

The portion sizes were absolutely microscopic.

Omission is when the author deliberately doesn't mention something that disagrees with, or disproves, their point of view.

Generalisations and **stereotypes** are when an author uses sweeping statements that aren't factually correct to support their argument.

The only thing teenagers care about are their phones.

Don't misspell 'biased' as 'biast'. It's an easy error to avoid.

Bias isn't always deliberate. Some authors might write in a biased way without realising it. If you spot biased writing, try to identify why an author might be biased. As a reader, you need to be able to identify the difference between fact and opinion.

Unbiased writing

Objective writing is the opposite of biased writing. This style of writing tries to present information in a neutral, factual way. It might include:

Counterarguments which acknowledge a different point of view, to make the author's opinion seem more balanced.

Although I don't agree with long-haul flights, I understand that sometimes they're necessary.

Unemotional language that sticks to the facts to keep the writing balanced and neutral.

The storm damaged 51 houses in the local area.

Quotes especially from experts or people affected by the issue.

Dr Jane Ross, an expert in nutrition, agrees, saying that "childhood obesity is a pressing concern for modern parents."

> Some writers of literary non-fiction may use similar linguistic techniques to fiction writers. Flick back to **pages 11–12** to remind yourself of some of these techniques.

Rhetorical devices

Writers may use **rhetorical devices** to make their text more convincing.

Rhetorical questions: questions that don't require an answer, but they make the reader think what their response might be. Writers often use them to encourage the reader to agree with them.	Who here has experienced overcrowding on trains?
Antithesis: a technique which contrasts two opposing ideas in the same sentence. It can be used to highlight the difference between two ideas.	One small step for man, one giant leap for mankind.
Parenthesis: describes an extra clause that has been inserted into a sentence. If the extra information is removed, the sentence would still make sense. Parenthesis is often separated by a pair of brackets, commas or dashes.	This notion, which is entirely absurd, should be stopped immediately.
List of three (also called **triplets**): describes three words or ideas that are put together for emphasis.	His suggestion is dangerous, impractical and illogical.

Humour

Writers use **humour** to try to get their readers on-side, and to make themselves seem more relatable.

Irony describes when a writer says something, but means the exact opposite. It can be used to create humour or sympathy with the reader.	Megan has the tough job of being a taste-tester at an ice cream factory.
Sarcasm is more aggressive than irony. It can be used to mock someone or something.	The team played absolutely brilliantly, missing chance after chance, and delighting fans with a skilful own goal.

Other language techniques

Emotive language aims to provoke a strong reaction from a reader. It's often used in texts that argue or persuade.	These tiny, helpless puppies have been cruelly abandoned.
Call to action is usually a command (see **page 14**) where you urge the reader to do something, for example to donate to a charity or share the article with someone who might find it helpful.	Write a letter to your MP asking for better public transport in your area.
Anecdotes are short personal stories that can be humorous or serious. Writers use them to create a relationship with the reader or to create a more intimate tone.	When I was a child, I wasn't allowed to put sugar on my cereal, and I've never forgiven my parents for this act of cruelty.

Source A is from a 19th-century guide about proper female behaviour.

Girls should be complimented for their modest bearing. One does not hear them talk about what they have done, or what they are going to do. They just do the thing and say nothing about it. They go about their business or pleasure quietly and gently, and never draw attention to themselves unnecessarily by behaving noisily and talking or laughing loudly in public. They should be particularly careful of this when in the company of boys or men.

Source B is from an article about female leadership written in 2016.

Girls, you have to be your own greatest champion, especially in a world where women's achievements are often unheard or undervalued. But this doesn't mean that you should bang your own drum so loudly that you drown out others: we should look to lift ourselves up, as well as those around us. Confidence and self-belief are important life skills for those looking to succeed in their chosen field, but don't overlook humility and kindness either.

You need to refer to **Source A** and **Source B** for this question.

Compare how the writers convey their different attitudes to female behaviour.

In your answer, you could:

- compare their different attitudes to female behaviour
- compare the methods the writers use to convey their attitudes
- support your response with references to both texts   **[16 marks]**

In Source A, the writer gives advice on how girls should behave, but their main concern is how 'improper' female behaviour can be perceived by others. The guide suggests that girls should be "modest" and should be especially careful about how they behave around boys or men, implying that men would find confident and outspoken women unpleasant and unattractive. However, Source B encourages girls to speak up and be their "own greatest champion" to improve their own "confidence and self-belief". The difference in attitudes is representative of the context when the sources were written. Women in the 19th century were expected to be polite and reserved, and subservient to men. Whereas today, women are permitted to have more self-confidence and they are considered equal to men.

Furthermore, Source A refers to women in the third person using the pronoun "they". This impersonal address conveys a haughty and judgemental tone, suggesting that the writer is distancing themselves from women, and implies that they are superior to the reader. Using the third person also suggests that the text is directed at both male and female readers, indicating that "boys or men" should also know what 'improper' behaviour looks like, so that they have the right to judge a woman who is not conforming to these standards. On the other hand, Source B is written in the second person, using the pronouns "you" and "we". The writer starts by addressing the readers as "Girls" which indicates that the writer is communicating directly to a female readership. This personal and inclusive tone suggests that the writer empathises with the reader and knows exactly how they are feeling. This helps to make the advice seem less patronising, as though it is coming from a friend.

This answer should be marked in accordance with the levels-based mark scheme on page 78.

 In the exam, the sources will be longer.

EXAMINATION PRACTICE

Source A is an extract from *The Englishwoman in America* by Isabella Bird, published in 1856. In it, Bird recalls a stormy sea voyage along the coast of Maine, USA.

I sat on deck till five, when I went down to my berth. As the evening closed in gloomily, the sea grew coarser, and I heard the captain say, "We are likely to have a very fresh night of it." Before I fell asleep, the mate put his head through the curtain to say, "It's a rough night, ladies, but there's no danger"; a left-handed way of giving courage, which of course frightened the timid. About eleven I was awoke by confused cries, and in my dawning consciousness everything seemed going to pieces. The curtain was undrawn, and I could see the hall continually swept by the waves.

Everything in our saloon was loose; rocking-chairs were careering about the floor and coming into collision; the stewardess, half-dressed, was crawling about from berth to berth, answering the inquiries of terrified ladies, and the ship was groaning and straining heavily; but I slept again, till awoke at midnight by a man's voice shouting "Get up, ladies, and dress, but don't come out till you're called; the gale's very heavy." Then followed a scene. People, helpless in illness a moment before, sprang out of their berths and hastily huddled in their clothes; mothers caught hold of their infants with a convulsive grasp; some screamed, others sat down in apathy, while not a few addressed agonised supplications to that God, too often neglected in times of health and safety, to save them in their supposed extremity.

Crash went the lamp, which was suspended from the ceiling, as a huge wave struck the ship, making her reel and stagger, and shrieks of terror followed this event, which left us in almost total darkness. Rush came another heavy wave, sweeping up the saloon, carrying chairs and stools before it, and as rapidly retiring. The hall was full of men, clinging to the supports, each catching the infectious fear from his neighbour. Wave after wave now struck the ship. I heard the captain say the sea was making a clean breach over her, and order the deck-load overboard. Shortly after, the water, sweeping in from above, put out the engine-fires, and, as she settled down continually in the trough of the sea, and lay trembling there as though she would never rise again, even in my ignorance I knew that she had "no way on her" and was at the mercy of the waters. I now understood the meaning of "blowing great guns." The wind sounded like continual discharges of heavy artillery, and the waves, as they struck the ship, felt like cannon-balls. I could not get up and dress, for, being in the top berth, I was unable to get out in consequence of the rolling of the ship, and so, being unable to mend matters, I lay quietly, the whole passing before me as a scene. I had several times been called on to anticipate death from illness; but here, as I heard the men outside say, "She's going down, she's water-logged, she can't hold together," there was a different prospect of sinking down among the long trailing weeds in the cold, deep waters of the Atlantic. Towards three o'clock, a wave, striking the ship, threw me against a projecting beam of the side, cutting my head severely and stunning me, and I remained insensible for three hours. We continued in great danger for ten hours, many expecting each moment to be their last, but in the morning the gale moderated, and by most strenuous exertions at the pumps the water was kept down till assistance was rendered, which enabled us about one o'clock to reach the friendly harbour of Portland in Maine, with considerable damage and both our boats stove. Deep thankfulness was expressed by many at such an unlooked-for termination of the night's terrors and adventures; many the resolutions expressed not to trust the sea again.

Source B is from an online article published in 2017. Here, the author describes her experiences of sailing her boat, *Genevieve,* through a storm.

As the skies overhead darkened into a sickly purple bruise, I stood transfixed and watched the storm approach. The nebulous, roiling clouds hastening towards me, unstoppable and inevitable. Realisation hit like a sucker punch, and my whole body went cold, with a gnawing dread pulling at my stomach.

There's nothing like being in the middle of the ocean to make you feel insignificant: *Genevieve* was just a tiny cork, floating along in the swell, completely at the mercy of mother nature. A well-timed hit along her starboard side and she could topple over as easily as a domino. There was no one else out here for miles. I was painfully, desperately alone.

What had started as a playful bob of the waves, soon became more violent as the wind picked up, and the sea began to churn. The splatter of spray hit the canvas like a drummer slapping a taut skin. Salt water poured into the cockpit, and I knew I had to make a decision, and quick. I could reef the sails, but doing this by myself in these conditions would be unmanageable at best, and dangerous at worst. Likewise, I could hoist the storm jib, but the sail was buried in a locker somewhere, and I simply didn't have time. Panicking, I decided my only option was to drop the sails and lie ahull. There was no point fighting against a more powerful foe.

I rapidly got to work, fingers fumbling in the cold, tugging at salt-slick knots. A deluge soon began, and it was impossible to say what was rain, and what was spray, as they lashed my face with equal vigour. *Genevieve* lurched, the waves lifting her to a crest, then slamming her into a trough. By some miracle, I managed to get the sails safely stowed.

Having done everything I could to secure *Genevieve* above deck, and fearful I could slide into the yawning water, I staggered down the companionway into the cabin. I slid into the safety of my bunk, grasping the rails with white knuckles, and lay drenched and shaking in the dim cocoon. *Genevieve* heaved and rolled, and the gale howled blue murder, the sound ricocheting off every surface. Flashes of lightning lit up the cabin and the foamy water through the porthole. I begged desperately for *Genevieve* to remain upright. My possessions rolled and rattled inside the lockers, thumping like an angry poltergeist demanding to be released. I suddenly realised that I was crying. Tears were streaming uncontrollably down my face. Was this where it all ended? Of all my foolhardy, reckless and impetuous actions, was this the one that ended it all?

1. For this question, you need to refer to the **whole of Source A**, with the **whole of Source B**.

   Compare how the writers convey their different perspectives and feelings about their experiences at sea.

   In your answer, you could:
   - compare their different perspectives and feelings.
   - compare the methods the writers use to convey their different perspectives and feelings.
   - support your answer with references to both texts

   [16 marks]

QUESTION 5 – EXAM TECHNIQUE

The final question on paper 2 tests your ability to write a piece of non-fiction.

Example question

05 'People seem to be concerned about the effects of climate change and global warming, but they're happy enough to go on holiday abroad and take long-haul flights which damage the environment. People shouldn't go on overseas holidays.'

Write a letter to the Minister for Transport in which you explain your point of view on this statement.

(24 marks for content and organisation
16 marks for technical accuracy)

[40 marks]

How to answer question 5

- This question covers AO5 and 6 (see **page xii** for a list of the AOs). It tests how well you can write clearly and effectively, and that you can suit your writing to different audiences and purposes.

- It also tests that you can structure your writing clearly, and that you can use different sentence structures and a wide vocabulary.

- This question also tests your spelling, punctuation and grammar. There are 16 marks available for technical accuracy.

- The question will give you an audience and purpose. In the example above you are writing a letter explaining your point of view, so you need to make sure that your writing is appropriate.

- It doesn't matter whether you agree with the statement or disagree with it. You should pick the side that you can write the most compelling case for.

- This question is worth 40 marks, and you should spend about 45 minutes on it. You should spend about 10 minutes on a plan, 25 minutes writing and 5-10 minutes checking and editing.

QUESTION 5 – WRITING A PLAN

The question will give you three important pieces of information: the **form**, the **purpose** and the **audience**. You need to adapt your writing to suit all three.

Form

Form describes the type of text, i.e. a letter, an article, a speech etc. Have a look at **pages 62–64** for more detail.

Purpose

This is the reason why you are writing the text, i.e. to argue, explain, persuade (see **page 42**).

Audience

This is who will be reading your text. It might be one person (i.e. a letter to someone specific) or a large group of people (i.e. an article for a newspaper). Have a look at **page 41** for more detail on audience.

Once you've established the form, audience and purpose, decide which structure and language techniques (see pages **54–56**) would be most suitable.

Structure

Your structure should be easy for the reader to follow.

1. You might want to start with an **introduction** where you clearly introduce your point of view.
2. Then, you could discuss each supporting point in a separate paragraph. A well-rounded answer would probably have 3–5 paragraphs, each with a distinct focus.
3. Finally, you could finish with a strong **conclusion** where you briefly summarise your key points and re-state your point of view, or you could end with a meaningful quote or a **call to action** (page 56)

> Make sure your introduction and conclusion match. It sounds obvious, but if you haven't planned your answer properly it can be easy to switch sides as you're writing.

Language techniques

You will need to select language techniques which are appropriate for your form, purpose and audience. For example, **alliteration** and **short sentences** would work well in a speech where the sound and pace of the text are important, whereas a **formal register** and an **impersonal tone** might be more appropriate for a letter to someone you don't know.

BEST FRIEND

QUESTION 5 — ARTICLES

Articles often come up in the exam, so make sure you're familiar with them.

Opinion pieces

As well as reporting on current events, newspapers also publish **opinion pieces** where writers discuss their point of view on a certain topic. If you're asked to write an article, it should include some of the features from **page 54–56**.

Articles

Different publications have different features and audiences.

Broadsheets

Broadsheets (e.g. *The Times* or *The Telegraph*) usually report on serious issues.

Language features
- Formal, impersonal **tone**
- Sophisticated language

Audience
- Readers are typically more educated, and interested in world affairs and politics.

Local / School newspapers

Local / School newspapers include stories that are specific to the local area or school. For example, a review about a school play.

Language features
- Less formal than a broadsheet

Audience
- Teachers, pupils and parents interested in what's happening at a school. Residents interested in local news.

Magazines

You might be more familiar with magazines that are aimed at a specific audience, for example football magazines aimed at readers who follow sport, or fashion magazines aimed at readers who are interested in shopping. However, some magazines include articles or opinion pieces similar to those found in newspapers. If you're asked to write a magazine article, it should be similar to a newspaper article.

You might also be asked to write an article to be published online. The language features and the audience will be very similar to print articles.

QUESTION 5 – LETTERS

You might not have much experience of writing letters, so it's worthwhile practising ahead of the exam in case you're asked to write one.

Audience

The reader of your letter might be someone very specific, like your headteacher or a friend, or it could be someone you don't know personally, like the Prime Minister. You might also need to write an **open letter** (a letter designed to be published and read by many people) or a letter to a specific group of people, such as students at your school.

You need to tailor your writing to match the person (or people) who will read the letter. If you are writing to someone you don't know or someone who is in a position of authority, you should use a **formal register**. If you're writing to someone you know or someone your own age, it might be more appropriate to use a chatty, **informal register**.

Features

Starting a letter

Letters usually start with a specific opening. For example, if you're writing a formal letter to someone you know, you could open with "Dear Mrs Travers". If it's a formal letter and you don't know the name of the person you are writing to, you could use "Dear Sir or Madam". If you're writing an open letter, you might use "Dear Class 7B" or "Dear library users", to indicate who the letter is addressed to.

Ending a letter

Letters usually have specific endings too. If you're writing a formal letter and you know the person you're writing too, you usually end "Yours sincerely". If you're writing a formal letter and you've addressed the letter to "Dear Sir or Madam", you usually end with "Yours faithfully".

If you're writing a letter to someone you know, it would be fine to end your letter with "Best wishes" or "From".

QUESTION 5 — SPEECHES

Speeches are designed to be read aloud, so think about how your speech would sound to an audience.

Speeches

Good speeches are powerful and exciting, they keep the audience interested and use linguistic techniques to encourage the audience to see the speaker's point of view. Here are some features that you could include in a speech:

Short sentences make a speech punchy and increase the **pace**.

Rhetorical questions involve the audience and encourage them to agree with the speaker's point of view.

Direct address (i.e. speaking directly to the audience using the pronoun 'you') makes the audience feel included.

Alliteration, **repetition** and **lists of three** can impact the **rhythm** of a speech and make key phrases more memorable.

Emotive language can provoke a reaction from the audience to make the speech more impactful.

A clear, easy-to-follow structure that builds to a **climax** helps the audience to focus on the main points and guide them to the overall purpose of the speech.

Remember to consider the audience of your speech, and tailor your language choices to make it more appropriate. A speech aimed at your classmates might use a more personal tone and more informal language, whereas a speech aimed at parents might use a more formal tone and less chatty language.

'Students' lives revolve around technology, and technology is the future. I think that all teaching and schoolwork should be done online.'

Write an article for the school newspaper in which you argue your point of view on this statement.

(24 marks for content and organisation and
16 marks for technical accuracy)

[40 marks]

Plan:

Audience: School newspaper readers, i.e. other students.

Language: Not too formal. Humour to get readers on-side.

Form: Newspaper article.

Purpose: Argue

Techniques: Rhetorical questions, humour, emotive language, lists of three, statistics, hyperbole.

Para 1 (intro): State point of view = disagree strongly.
(The suggestion that all schoolwork should be done online is impractical, misguided and outrageous.)

Para 2: Not everyone has access to the Internet / technology — disadvantages some students.
(Why should some pupils' education have to suffer?)

Para 3: Technology is unreliable — laptops can break, and Internet can go down.
(Technology can be as reliable as a paper umbrella.)

Para 4: Student wellbeing – pupils may become isolated.
(62% of students would be lonely if they didn't come into class)

Para 5: Quality of learning may suffer if unsupervised.
(Putting students back in the classroom under the direct supervision of teachers is the only way to keep pupils focused.)

Para 5 (concl): Sum up argument.
(It simply isn't a realistic replacement for in-school learning.)

The example answer is on the next page.

If you run out of time, the examiner may look at your plan to see what you would have written, and you may be able to get a few extra marks. Make sure your plan is legible and don't scribble it out.

When I heard someone say that all teaching and schoolwork should be done online, I laughed. It had to be a joke, right? The thought that schoolwork should be done solely online is impractical, misguided, and outrageous, and anyone who thinks moving all learning online is the right course of action must not know students at all. Let me set the record straight.

Firstly, not all students have access to computers, let alone the Internet. Moving to an online classroom would massively disadvantage any student who doesn't have the right equipment. It's ludicrous that pupils should have to face this inequality. Even in homes where there is access to the Internet and a computer, what happens if there aren't enough computers for each student? Are siblings expected to take turns? I don't think so.

Secondly, everyone knows how unreliable technology can be. Laptops can glitch, the internet can fail, webcams can break. As useful as technology can be, it can also be as reliable as a paper umbrella in a downpour. Even if technology isn't actually broken, pupils can still use it as an excuse not to attend online lessons. "My webcam is broken" is the new "my dog ate my homework."

Thirdly, has anyone thought what effect online schooling might have on student wellbeing? Trapped inside all day with just a flickering monitor for company, pupils will become isolated from their friends. In fact, 62% of pupils surveyed said that they would feel lonely if they didn't come into school for classes. That's almost two thirds of the student body. We can't betray these people by switching to online learning.

Most importantly, the quality of online learning just doesn't compare to in-class teaching. Who here hasn't been distracted by their phone or their pet or their games console when they should have been paying attention? While shirking schoolwork and getting distracted seems like a more appealing option in the short term, we're only hurting ourselves in the long term. When exams roll around and we've spent hours scrolling through cat videos and memes rather than revising, we'll only have ourselves to blame. Putting students back in the classroom under the direct supervision of teachers is the only way to keep pupils focused.

While I agree that home learning occasionally has its benefits, and it can be an adequate alternative when pupils can't make it into school due to illness, it simply isn't a realistic replacement for in-school learning. Anyone who thinks that either doesn't care about the quality of students' education or doesn't care about the welfare of students.

This answer should be marked in accordance with the levels-based mark scheme on page 75–77.

EXAMINATION PRACTICE

1. 'Social media is pointless, shallow and damages young people's mental health. I believe that only people aged over 18 should be allowed to have social media accounts.'

    Write an article for a broadsheet in which you explain your point of view on this statement.

    (24 marks for content and organisation
    16 marks for technical accuracy)
    [40 marks]

2. 'Students waste their time at school learning things that won't help them when they're older. Schools should spend more time teaching students practical life skills like how to maintain a car and how to budget their money."

    Write a letter to your headteacher arguing your point of view on this statement.

    (24 marks for content and organisation
    16 marks for technical accuracy)
    [40 marks]

EXAMINATION PRACTICE ANSWERS

1. Any four from the following:
    The spider is asleep.
    The spider is ugly.
    The spider's body is covered in coarse hair.
    The spider's body is covered in black hair.
    The spider has a row of sharp teeth. / The spider's teeth are sharp.
    The spider's teeth are a foot long.
    The spider's body is pudgy / fat.
    The spider had a slender neck.

2. Any four from the following:
    The storeroom is damp.
    The storeroom had been in an old farmhouse.
    The is no carpet in the storeroom.
    The floor of the storeroom is uneven.
    It is dark / "black as pitch" in the storeroom.
    The windows of the storeroom are shuttered.
    The walls of the storeroom are lined with boxes and/or barrels and/or sacks.
    The storeroom smells like mould.

3. Any four from the following:
    The sled didn't have runners.
    The sled is made from stout wood.
    The sled is made from birch-bark.
    The sled is on snowy ground.
    The sled is designed to travel on snow.
    The front of the sled is shaped like a scroll.
    The sled has an item tied on top of it.
    The sled has an oblong box on it.

1. The writer uses language to describe the scene as beautiful and mysterious, but they also hint at something darker too. The writer uses the simile "like a white-clad girl tip-toeing" to describe the plum tree leaning out to the water which conjures the image of an angel or fairy, reinforcing the scene as magical and enchanting. Furthermore, the colour of the water is described as "ethereal", "spiritual" and "elusive". The cumulative effect of these adjectives implies that the water is changing colour in an almost magical way. These colours have "no name" which adds to their mystery since the reader cannot picture what they look like.

    The sentence order guides the reader's focus, introducing all the landscape features one by one, and the writer uses long compound and complex sentences to describe the features which slows the pace of the text, and creates a calm and peaceful tone. The long sentences also make the reader feel as though they are on a long journey with the characters as they travel steadily through the landscape.

    Although the writer presents the scene as beautiful and mysterious, it is also slightly unsettling as there is mention of darkness too. The fir and maple trees are "darkly translucent" in their "shadows", which suggests that there is potentially something sinister lurking in the dark. This feeling of disquiet is also reinforced by the frogs' "mournfully-sweet chorus", reinforcing the juxtaposition of sadness and beauty. This creates a sense of trepidation in the reader, as they do not know whether the characters are heading into danger.

2. The writer uses language to create a comfortable and inviting atmosphere in the kitchen by using adjectives from the semantic field of happiness. The benches are "cheerful", and the firelight is "merry", while alliteration in the phrase "comfort and contentment" emphasises that guests to the kitchen will receive a warm welcome.

    The writer repeats the adjective "plain" to describe the kitchen and the food, which suggests that the kitchen is humble, but the benches, which are "shiny with long wear", suggest that the kitchen welcomes lots of guests. This presents the kitchen as an unpretentious, sociable place.

The repetition of personification in the final sentence, including "the benches ... exchanged cheerful glances" and "the brick floor smiled" suggest that even the inanimate objects in the kitchen are friendly and welcoming. This final sentence is especially long, using semi-colons in place of full stops to slow the pace, and reinforce the cosy, comfortable tone. This long, descriptive sentence also makes the kitchen feel full as the personification animates the furniture in the kitchen, making it feel lively and welcoming.

Paper 1, Section A: Question 3

The extract is written in the third person and has a chronological, linear structure. This allows the reader to follow the main character, Mrs Wilton, and experience the events unfolding along with her. The writer structures the story to slowly reveal information to the reader, and this anticipation builds narrative tension and keeps the reader engaged.

At the start of the extract, the writer focuses the reader's attention on a mysterious scene. The writer introduces Mrs Wilton, who is behaving suspiciously. She is described as walking "slowly" and "anxiously", suggesting that she is uneasy and anticipating something. This creates tension as the reader wants to know why she is anxious. This uneasy feeling is increased as Mrs Wilton pulls "her furs closer round her". This defensive behaviour suggests that Mrs Wilton is protecting herself from something, which makes the reader fear for Mrs Wilton's safety. This mysterious opening acts as a narrative hook, as it grabs the reader's attention and makes them invested in the story.

The writer then reveals that Mrs Wilton is looking for an antiques shop, but the description of the shop adds to the reader's feeling of unease. The window is described as "shabby", "uncleaned" with "an unassorted heap of things". This suggests that the antique shop is neglected, but the juxtaposition of the neglect with the description that many of the items are "of great value" makes the reader feel mistrustful of the shop. When Mrs Wilton confirms, "Yes; this is the place", the reader feels wary that the shop might be unsafe, and intrigued as to why Mrs Wilton is visiting it, as she has been looking specifically for this unappealing and ominous shop.

The writer then focuses the reader's attention on the inside of the antiques shop, which adds to the unsettling mood. The door opens with an "ill-tempered jangle" which implies that the antiques shop is not a welcoming place. This uneasy tone is heightened when the owner is described as "cunning". This suggests that he knows more than he is letting on, which makes the reader concerned for Mr Wilton, and adds to the building tension.

The antiques dealer speaks to Mrs Wilton but the dialogue is one-sided. This speech helps to further the plot, but it also continues the mysterious tone, as the antiques dealer seemingly knows why Mrs Wilton is there, without her ever needing to explain. This increases the suspense as the characters know more than the reader. The extract ends with a cliffhanger as the reader follows Mrs Wilton up the "dark" stairs, not knowing what she might encounter.

Paper 1, Section A: Question 4

I partially agree with the student's statement, as I think both the children and Abbie are deserving of our sympathy. Abbie clearly loves the orange tree. She is fascinated by it as she watches it grow "day by day", looking forward to the day the orange becomes "large and yellow". She enjoys just being in its presence, and she gladly does chores because it gives her "something extra to do near the orange tree." The love she has for the tree means that she spends weeks tending to it, even creeping down the "cold, bare halls" to put "an extra chunk of hardwood into the stove" to make sure that it stays warm. This shows how she nurtures the orange, almost as if it is a person, making sure that it has the optimum conditions to thrive. Abbie has a servant, yet she happily cleans and fetches firewood to make sure that the orange tree gets the best possible care. The writer includes all this detail to build a clear picture of Abbie's love for the orange-tree in the reader's mind. This description also suggests that Abbie is lonely, and she focuses all her attention on the orange tree because she has no-one else to love. When the orange is "snipped" from the tree, the reader feels a great deal of sympathy for Abbie. All the care and affection she has put into growing the orange is ruined in an instant. The orange is more than a piece of fruit to Abbie: the orange gives her life purpose and something to care and nurture. Additionally, Bruce cutting the orange is especially hurtful because Abbie invites the children into her home to give them "cookies" and she generously lets them take fruit from "the yard". Her kindness to the children is repaid in betrayal, which generates even more sympathy for Abbie.

Although the reader feels sympathy for Abbie, the children deserve some sympathy too. Although Bruce Sanders cuts the orange from the tree, all the children are punished for his actions. Abbie lashes out at "the two children nearest" and shakes them. The children are also driven off her property and she decides never to let them come into her yard again. It seems unfair that all the children are penalised for one person's actions. Although it was wrong of Bruce to cut the orange from the tree, especially since he had been warned "don't you dare touch it", he wasn't to know how much love and attention had gone into cultivating the orange, especially since the children are also allowed to take "fruit from the trees" in Abbie's yard, so there is a precedence for taking Abbie's fruit. However, when Bruce cuts the orange the other children are "unnaturally still" which shows that they know that they have done something wrong. Once the children have left Abbie's house, they yell her name, almost taunting her, which shows that they do not feel remorse for their actions, which creates even more sympathy for Abbie.

1. If you stumbled across Wolf Creek, you would be forgiven for thinking it was a mirage. Three days from the nearest town, it shifted and shimmered in the midday heat, marooned in a sea of sand. If you happened to roll in from the west, you'd be met with the saloon. A thumping, thrumming place, where the patrons were always thirsty, the girls were always lively and the music was always loud. Sure, the whiskey was watered down, the piano was out of tune, and the deck of cards always seemed to have more than four aces, but no one seemed to care too much, because their purses were full and there was nowhere else to go. If you took the creaky flight of stairs to the first floor, you would find four small rooms to rent. Guests were lucky to fall asleep before 4 am, what with all the ruckus downstairs, but for saddle-sore men who hadn't seen an eiderdown for months, a warm bed and protection from the elements was like resting on a cloud in heaven.

    If you exited the saloon and hung a left, you'd find the General Store, where ruddy-cheeked Ma Stout in a checked dress and starch-stiff apron would hawk barrels of corn and jars of jerky. You had to keep a look out for weevils in your flour, but in truth, many would take their chances with the weevils over Ma Stout. Men would tie their horses out front, and the bigger beasts would pull and stamp, loosening the joists in the soft dirt so that the rickety veranda was always on a bit of an angle. If a storm blew in from the desert, little mounds of sand would pile up like turrets.

    Oh, there was a doctor too, if you went just a little way beyond the fork in the road. He was more likely to be found in the saloon than his practice, but no one could suck the venom from a snake bite as well as the Doc, regardless of how many whiskeys he'd had. He once saved a man from a coyote bite that had gone so deep you could see the bone. Turns out alcohol is good for flushing out infection.

    In its heyday of the gold rush, Wolf Creek had been a prosperous place. Of course, with prosperity, came trouble. Not just the usual sorts of trouble, drunks, layabouts, petty thieves, but a worse sort of trouble. Trouble that poisoned the town and left too many poor souls in the churchyard. It was this trouble that killed Wolf Creek and left it an empty, rotting, husk.

2. I was nine years old when we abandoned our home. Old enough to remember some things, but too young for others. The overwhelming emotion when we left was fear, yawning, biting, gnawing fear. The shelling had been intermittent for weeks. Bombs were targeting a nearby chemical factory, which was far enough away that my mother was prepared to stay. Plenty of other families in our apartment complex were staying put too: women, the elderly and the young. All the men were fighting at the front, so leaving felt like a betrayal. Our men were so brave, yet we would scurry like frightened mice at the sound of a bomb 3 miles away. If we left our homes, what if our fathers, husbands and brothers returned to find their homes an empty shell? It would suggest that we were happy for them to face danger, but not ourselves. Of course, there were the practicalities of leaving. We could only take what we could carry, and for some, that was very little. It was a choice between the uncertainty of the bombs, or the certainty of facing a harsh winter with no home.

    One night, the moon hung like a fishing hook in the sky, thin, delicate, silvery. The bombing came closer. The sky lit up, as if dawn had come early, but instead of birdsong there was an echoing, booming, thunderous roar. My mother, dressed in her nightgown, came into my room. She held my small hands in hers and whispered urgently.

    "Pack a bag. Only bring what you can carry. Mittens, a hat. Your scarf. Spare socks." I don't know why her voice was so low, it was almost drowned out by the noise. She held my face in her hands and kissed my head, before leaving just as suddenly. I pulled on my jeans, a sweater, thick socks and a coat. I haphazardly pulled my gloves, scarf and hat from my wardrobe and stuffed them inside my backpack. My bag was so small, it was almost full with these few meagre possessions. I went into the kitchen, where my mother was emptying packets and tins from the cupboard into a suitcase, trying to make them fit with shaky hands. She too was in jeans and a coat, now.

    "Hurry, hurry." She said as another false dawn flashed and the windowpanes rattled.

    We went to the door and my mother fumbled with her keys.

    "Is there any point in locking the door behind us?" She laughed darkly. "If it's all blown to smithereens, then what good will a lock do?" She locked it anyway. We met others in the stairwell, scurrying like ants; clasping backpacks, suitcases, shopping bags. The niceties we swapped with our neighbours were gone, replaced with urgent pushing and sharp elbows. I couldn't see above the tide of people sloshing down the stairwell, until the wave broke at the entrance and people spilled like foam on the concrete outside, scattering in all directions. My mother grabbed my hand and pulled me into the woods that surrounded the apartment building, following some unseen trail to safety.

You should have selected:
    A   The clerk was friendly.
    C   The rooms on the top floor are less likely to be damp.
    F   The glass doors in Nellie's room provide the only ventilation.
    G   Nellie's room had a balcony

Source A describes the market as being charming, where visitors can experience "Christmas magic" and "cutesy little wooden huts". There are plenty of attractions for children, for example the "gilded carousel" and the "penny arcade", which implies that the market is designed to be welcoming and family friendly. On the other hand, the market in Source B is presented as dangerous and unappealing. The people at the market are "brawling", "cursing" and described as a "quarrelsome crowd". This implies that the market isn't safe or pleasant, especially for children who would be exposed to "coarse wit" and "vulgar and improper songs".

Another difference between the two markets is that the market in Source A is presented as a place where people with disposable income can spend money. The items on sale ("fudge", "toys", "doughnuts") aren't essential, and it's implied that the prices at the market are expensive. For example, the pick 'n' mix has an "eye-watering mark-up" and the penny arcade "will leave your wallet much lighter". Contrastingly, the market in Source B is a place where poor people can buy essential items, for example "stale fish, and stale vegetables". The people shopping at the market are "the poorest of the poor" and the people selling items are also impoverished, as they are described as "eager, pushing, poor".

The writer uses language to suggest that the mountains are dangerous and menacing. They achieve this in the first paragraph by describing a sunset, which is usually presented as beautiful, as something sinister, for example, the image of the "line of shadow" creeping up the mountainside. This image of encroaching darkness fills the reader with a sense of foreboding, suggesting that a change is coming over the mountain. This is continued when the writer describes how the sunset glinting off the mountains' peaks "paled and died". This mention of death creates an uneasy feeling in the reader, as if the mountain is something to be feared.

The writer continues this feeling of fear by using personification, for example "the ice cliffs yawn pitilessly". This suggests that the fissures are like a mouth, which will show no mercy and may swallow unprepared mountaineers. This personification is extended when the writer says, "Sometimes [the mountains] seem to smile, but their welcome... is treacherous and cruel." This suggests that the mountains lure mountaineers with a welcome smile, but that they are enticing people into a dangerous trap. This makes the reader feel as though the mountains' actions are deliberate, and that they enjoy causing harm. This presents them as monstrous.

The writer also implies the mountains are something more powerful than humanity. The mountains' "resources are endless" and their "ally is the storm". This suggests that the mountains are an almost invincible foe, who could easily destroy any mountaineers. This reinforces the idea that the mountains are dangerous and threatening.

The writer of Source A gives the impression that she is relatively calm about the voyage in the storm, which is startling because she describes a potentially life-threatening journey. The writer uses an impersonal, detached tone, and narrates the situation almost as if she were an onlooker, focusing on the other passengers' reactions, rather than expressing her own feelings. When the storm hits, the writer describes the scene in an objective way. She recognises the chaos that surrounds her, but is unaffected by what she sees. For example, she describes the stewardess "crawling" about the cabins, which implies that the motion of the boat is so violent that crew members, who likely have experience of choppy seas, are unable stand. Furthermore, this image of a woman crawling along the floor also conveys a pitiful desperation that is echoed by the "terrified" people on the boat. However, the writer describes that the "rolling of the ship" causes her to "lay quietly" in her bunk, implying that she seems almost apathetic to the situation, and isn't affected by the "infectious fear" experienced by the other passengers. The writer conveys the seriousness of the situation by personifying the boat as "groaning" and "straining". This description suggests that the boat is struggling to remain afloat and that it could sink at any moment. The writer extends this personification later in the passage where she describes the boat as "trembling", which suggests that even the boat is petrified and helpless in the face of the storm. This description helps the reader to imagine the severity of the situation, which contrasts with the writer's calm attitude. Even when the writer thinks that the boat could sink, she remains impassive, and describes "sinking down amongst the long trailing weeds" without any hint of hysteria or fear. The writer's indifference could be because she is a passenger on the ship, so she is dependent on the crew to navigate the boat to safety, and since the writer is "unable to mend matters", she is resigned to her fate.

In contrast, the writer of Source B is dependent on herself to survive the storm, admitting that she is "painfully, desperately alone", so she expresses much stronger emotions than writer of Source B. The author describes her feelings about the oncoming storm using the simile "Realisation hit like a sucker punch". This effectively conveys her reaction, as the reader can image the visceral sensation of being punched in the stomach and the resulting sensation of shock. The writer compares the boat to a "tiny cork" and describes how the boat could "topple over as easily as a domino". This makes the boat seem insignificant compared to the storm and the ocean, and makes the reader feel anxious for the writer and her perilous situation. The writer of Source B gives the impression of being desperate and frenzied as she secures the boat. She works "rapidly", and describes her "fingers fumbling", this alliteration reinforces her panic, and her frantic actions as she races against the clock to prepare Genevieve. The author uses verbs such as "staggered", "slid" and "grasping" to show how little control she has over her movement, and how desperate and dangerous the situation is. Like the author of Source A, the writer goes to lie in her bunk, but where Isabella Bird is able to sleep, the author of Source B lies "drenched and shaking" and begins to cry, which demonstrates her hopelessness. At the end of the passage, the writer uses rhetorical questions ("Was this where it all ended?") to show her anxiety and despair. These questions also reinforce her feeling of uncertainty, as she doesn't know if the boat will survive the storm.

1. Social Media has exploded over the past 15 years, and many teenagers have grown up surrounded by online platforms: Twitter, Snapchat, Instagram, and of course, Tik Tok. Social media often comes under fire from its opponents, most recently for being shallow and for damaging young people's mental health. While I agree that social media is far from perfect, restricting access to over 18s would be a terrible loss for younger users.

   Perhaps most importantly, social media is a space where young people can seek refuge, especially those individuals who might be bullied or marginalised. Social media can provide a welcoming, safe community for those discovering their identity and individuality. To be surrounded by like-minded people, free from judgement, can help young people's mental health enormously. It's not just marginalised groups who benefit. No matter what you're interested in, whether it's sport, music or fashion, there are thousands of other users you can connect with to explore and discuss your hobbies and interests. Creating close, meaningful relationships is one of the best ways young people can improve their mental health.

   Secondly, social media isn't just silly dances and lip syncing, there's also a more worthy side to social media too. Social media is a way for young people to learn about activism, and how they can make a difference. Online communities are a great way to mobilise young people and to get them to care about things that really matter: equality, the environment and democracy. Young people can use social media to share petitions, spread the word about marches and protests, or just as a platform to voice our opinions. Sometimes our generation is slammed for being 'woke', overly sensitive to issues, but in truth, we've had our eyes opened to the inequality that surrounds us, in part thanks to social media, and we're prepared to speak out against injustice.

   Thirdly, social media allows young people to connect with others from all over the world. Before social media, young people were more restricted in who they interacted with, often confined to people in their local area. This meant that young people were in danger of growing up with a limited perspective, strongly influenced by the thoughts and opinions of the people who surrounded them. Now, social media has given young people the thoughts and opinions of people from all over the world, and allows them to become better informed and more well-rounded individuals.

   Furthermore, I believe that restricting access to under-18s would be very difficult to put into practice. Most young people are tech-savvy enough to know that age restrictions can be easily bypassed, and that introducing age-verification checks would not be adequate to stop young people from creating accounts. If nothing else, trying to stop under-18s on social media would be futile.

   Admittedly, social media isn't perfect. There's a lot of pressure on young people to look a certain way, and this shallow side of social media can impact young people's mental health. For the millions of users who use social media to inspire, create and connect, there will always be a handful who use it to bully and abuse. Even if access was restricted to over 18s, those trolls will still find a way hurt other users. So instead of removing under-18s, social media corporations should take more responsibility for making their platforms a safe and welcoming space, where users' wellbeing is put ahead of profit.

2. Dear Ms Irving,

   I am writing to you to ask you to reconsider the curriculum at our school. While there is a place for an academic education, and much of what we learn in school is very valuable, I strongly believe that practical skills, such as budgeting, car maintenance and childcare, should also be on the timetable to prepare students for real life outside the walls of the classroom.

   Firstly, think of all the time, resources and money spent teaching students how to apply Pythagoras' Theorem; and for what? So that they can answer a question on their GCSE Maths paper? Beyond that, I would go out on a limb to say that almost no-one uses Pythagoras' Theorem once they leave the classroom. Instead, during Maths lessons, schools should teach students things they will need for adult life: managing money, creating a budget, taxes and mortgages. These skills will be far more useful than knowing how to solve quadratic equations, and will encourage students to become financially responsible adults.

   Secondly, the education system is currently biased in favour of those wanting to go on to further study and higher education. While the academically gifted may want to know the finer points of imagery in the works of Charles Dickens, this has no practical use whatsoever for those of us who want to enter the world of work. For those of us who are more interested in employment than university, lessons on car maintenance would be far more useful. Being able to commute to work in a safe, well-maintained vehicle would be much more worthwhile than learning about similes and metaphors. Vehicle maintenance would also help to keep our roads safer and reduce the likelihood of accidents. Surely that has more merit than spotting personification in a poem?

   Thirdly, the vast majority of pupils at this school will become parents someday. Isn't it a huge oversight that we are taught nothing about how to look after children or raise a family? Who will teach us how to change a nappy or burp a baby? Caring for and raising another human life is an enormous responsibility, and one that many people are not fully prepared for. Clearly, more people will benefit from being taught about childcare than being taught about the atomic number of sodium.

   Mrs Irving, I hope that you read this letter and see how valuable it would be to teach young people the skills they need to succeed in life, rather than adhering to an outdated curriculum that only benefits those who choose further education.

   Yours sincerely,

   Mohameed Khan

LEVELS-BASED MARK SCHEMES FOR EXTENDED RESPONSE QUESTIONS

Questions that require extended writing use mark bands. The whole answer will be marked together to determine which mark band it fits into and which mark should be awarded within the mark band.

The descriptors have been written in simple language to give an indication of the expectations of each mark band. See the AQA website for the official mark schemes used.

Paper 1, Question 2

Level 4 (7–8 marks)	• Shows insightful and detailed understanding of language. • Analyses the effects of the writer's choice of language. • Selects a range of appropriate and thoughtful quotes and examples. • Makes sophisticated and accurate use of subject terminology.
Level 3 (5–6 marks)	• Shows clear understanding of language. • Explains clearly the effects of the writer's choice of language. • Selects a range of relevant quotes and examples. • Makes clear and accurate use of subject terminology.
Level 2 (3–4 marks)	• Shows some understanding of language. • Attempts to comment on the effect of language. • Selects some appropriate quotes and examples. • Makes some use of subject terminology.
Level 1 (1–2 marks)	• Shows simple awareness of language. • Offers simple comment on the effect of language. • Selects simple quotes and examples. • Makes simple use of subject terminology.
0 marks	• No answer has been given or the answer given makes no relevant points.

Paper 1, Question 3

Level 4 (7–8 marks)	• Shows insightful and detailed understanding of structural features. • Analyses the effects of the writer's choice of structural features. • Selects a range of appropriate and thoughtful quotes and examples. • Makes sophisticated and accurate use of subject terminology.
Level 3 (5–6 marks)	• Shows clear understanding of structural features. • Explains clearly the effects of the writer's choice of structural features. • Selects a range of relevant quotes and examples. • Makes clear and accurate use of subject terminology.

| Level 2
(3–4 marks) | • Shows some understanding of structural features.
• Attempts to comment on the effect of structural features.
• Selects some appropriate quotes and examples.
• Makes some use of subject terminology. |
|---|---|
| Level 1
(1–2 marks) | • Shows simple awareness of structural features.
• Offers simple comment on the effect of structure.
• Selects simple quotes and examples.
• Makes simple use of subject terminology. |
| 0 marks | • No answer has been given or the answer given makes no relevant points. |

Paper 1, Question 4

| Level 4
(16–20 marks) | • Shows perceptive and detailed evaluation.
• Evaluates critically and in detail the effect(s) on the reader.
• Shows perceptive understanding of the writer's methods.
• Selects a range of appropriate and thoughtful quotes and examples.
• Develops a convincing and critical response to the focus of the statement. |
|---|---|
| Level 3
(11–15 marks) | • Shows a clear and relevant evaluation.
• Evaluates clearly the effect(s) on the reader.
• Shows clear understanding of the writer's methods.
• Selects a range of relevant quotes and examples.
• Makes a clear and relevant response to the focus of the statement. |
| Level 2
(6–10 marks) | • Shows some attempts at evaluation.
• Makes some evaluative comment(s) on effect(s) on the reader.
• Shows some understanding of the writer's methods.
• Selects a some appropriate quotes and examples.
• Makes some response to the focus of the statement. |
| Level 1
(1–5 marks) | • Shows simple, limited evaluation.
• Makes simple, limited evaluative comment(s) on effect(s) on the reader.
• Shows limited understanding of the writer's methods.
• Selects simple, limited quotes and examples.
• Makes a simple, limited response to the focus of the statement. |
| 0 marks | • No answer has been given or the answer given makes no relevant points. |

Paper 1 and Paper 2, Question 5 (Content and organisation)

Upper Level 4 **(22–24 marks)**	**Content** • Communication is convincing and compelling. • Tone, style and register are assuredly matched to purpose and audience. • Extensive and ambitious vocabulary with sustained crafting of linguistic devices. **Organisation** • Varied and inventive use of structural features. • Writing is compelling, incorporating a range of convincing and complex ideas. • Fluently linked paragraphs with seamlessly integrated discourse markers.
Lower Level 4 **(19–21 marks)**	**Content** • Communication is convincing. • Tone, style and register are convincingly matched to purpose and audience. • Extensive vocabulary with conscious crafting of linguistic devices. **Organisation** • Varied and effective use of structural features. • Writing is highly engaging, with a range of developed complex ideas. • Consistently coherent use of paragraphs with integrated discourse markers.
Upper Level 3 **(16–18 marks)**	**Content** • Communication is consistently clear. • Tone, style and register are clearly and consistently matched to purpose and audience. • Increasingly sophisticated vocabulary and phrasing, chosen for effect with a range of successful linguistic devices. **Organisation** • Effective use of structural features. • Writing is engaging, using a range of clear, connected ideas. • Coherent paragraphs with integrated discourse markers.
Lower Level 3 **(13–15 marks)**	**Content** • Communication is generally clear. • Tone, style and register are generally matched to purpose and audience. • Vocabulary clearly chosen for effect and appropriate use of linguistic devices **Organisation** • Usually effective use of structural features • Writing is engaging, with a range of connected ideas. • Usually coherent paragraphs with a range of discourse markers.
Upper Level 2 **(10–12 marks)**	**Content** • Communicates with some sustained success. • Some sustained attempt to match tone, style and register to purpose and audience. • Conscious use of vocabulary with some use of linguistic devices. **Organisation** • Some use of structural features. • Increasing variety of linked and relevant ideas. • Some use of paragraphs and some use of discourse markers.

Lower Level 2 (7–9 marks)	**Content** • Communicates with some success. • Attempts to match tone, style and register to purpose and audience. • Begins to vary vocabulary with some use of linguistic devices. **Organisation** • Attempts to use structural features. • Some linked and relevant ideas. • Attempt to write in paragraphs with some discourse markers, not always appropriate.
Upper Level 1 (4–6 marks)	**Content** • Communicates simply. • Simple awareness of matching tone, style and register to purpose and audience. • Simple vocabulary; simple linguistic devices. **Organisation** • Evidence of simple structural features. • One or two relevant ideas, simple linked. • Random paragraph structure.
Lower Level 1 (1–3 marks)	**Content** • Limited communication. • Occasional sense of matching tone, style and register to purpose and audience. • Simple vocabulary **Organisation** • Limited or no evidence of structural features • One or two unlinked ideas. • No paragraphs.
0 marks	• No answer has been given or the answer given makes no relevant points.

Paper 1 and Paper 2, Question 5 (Spelling, punctuation and grammar)

Level 4 (13–16 marks)	• Sentence demarcation is consistently secure and consistently accurate. • Wide range of punctuation is used with a high-level of accuracy. • Uses a full range of appropriate sentence forms for effect. • Uses Standard English consistently and appropriately with secure control of complex grammatical structures. • High level of accuracy in spelling, including ambitious vocabulary • Extensive and ambitious use of vocabulary
Level 3 (9–12 marks)	• Sentence demarcation is mostly secure and mostly accurate • Range of punctuation is used, mostly with success • Uses a variety of sentence forms for effect • Mostly uses Standard English appropriately with mostly controlled grammatical structures • Generally accurate spelling, including complex and irregular words • Increasingly sophisticated use of vocabulary

Level 2 (5–8 marks)	• Sentence demarcation is mostly secure and sometimes accurate • Some control of a range of punctuation • Attempts a variety of sentence forms • Some use of Standard English with some control of agreement • Some accurate spelling of more complex words • Varied use of vocabulary
Level 1 (1–4 marks)	• Occasional use of sentence demarcation • Some evidence of conscious punctuation • Simple range of sentence forms • Occasional use of Standard English with limited control of agreement • Accurate basic spelling • Simple use of vocabulary
0 marks	• Students' spelling, punctuation and grammar is sufficiently poor to prevent understanding or meaning

Paper 2, Question 2

Level 4 (7–8 marks)	• Makes perceptive inferences from both texts • Makes thoughtful references and/or use of details from the text which are relevant to the question. • Shows thoughtful similarities between the texts.
Level 3 (5–6 marks)	• Makes clear inferences from both texts • Selects clear references and/or use of details from the text which are relevant to the question. • Shows clear similarities between the texts.
Level 2 (3–4 marks)	• Attempts some inference(s) from one/both texts. • Selects some appropriate references and/or use of details from one/both texts. • Shows some similarities between the texts.
Level 1 (1–2 marks)	• Uses paraphrased information rather than inferences. • Selects simple reference(s) or details from the text from one/both texts. • Shows simple similarities between the texts.
0 marks	• No answer has been given or the answer given makes no relevant points.

Paper 2, Question 3

Level 4 **(10–12 marks)**	• Analyses the effects of the writer's choices of language. • Selects a range of thoughtful textual detail. • Makes sophisticated and accurate use of subject terminology.
Level 3 **(7–9 marks)**	• Clearly explains the effects of the writer's choice of language. • Selects a range of relevant textual detail. • Makes clear and accurate use of subject terminology.
Level 2 **(4–6 marks)**	• Attempts to comment on the effect of language. • Selects some appropriate textual detail. • Makes some use of subject terminology, mainly appropriately.
Level 1 **(1–3 marks)**	• Offers simple comment on the effect of language. • Selects simple reference(s) or detail(s) from the text. • Makes simple use of subject terminology, not always appropriately.
0 marks	• No answer has been given or the answer given makes no relevant points.

Paper 2, Question 4

Level 4 **(13–16 marks)**	• Analyses how writers' methods are used. • Selects a range of thoughtful supporting detail from both texts. • Shows a detailed and perceptive understanding of the different ideas and perspectives in both texts.
Level 3 **(9–12 marks)**	• Clearly explains how writers' methods are used. • Selects relevant detail to support both texts. • Shows a clear understanding of the different ideas and perspectives in both texts.
Level 2 **(5–8 marks)**	• Makes some comment on how writers' methods are used. • Selects some appropriate details from one or both texts, not always supporting. • Shows some understanding of different ideas and perspectives.
Level 1 **(1–4 marks)**	• Makes simple identification of writers' methods. • Selects simple details from one or both texts. • Shows simple awareness of ideas and/or perspectives.
0 marks	• No answer has been given or the answer given makes no relevant points.

If you're looking for the levels-based mark scheme for Q5 for Paper 2, turn to pages 75–77. The mark scheme is identical to that used for Q5, Paper 1.

INDEX

0–9

19th-century texts 39

A

adjectives 8
adverbs 8
alliteration 11, 64
analogy 12
anecdotes 56
anti-climax 21
antithesis 56
apostrophes viii
articles 62
assessment objectives xii
audience 41, 61, 63

B

bias 42, 55
broadsheets 62

C

call to action 56
capital letters viii
characters 2, 30
chronological order 19
cinematic writing 19
clauses 15, 39
clichés 31
cliffhangers 21
climax 21, 64
colloquial language 54
colons ix
commands 14
commas viii
connotations 9
context 40
correcting mistakes xi
counterarguments 55

D

descriptions 32
determiners 8
direct address 41, 42, 54
direct speech ix, 21
double negatives x

E

editing x
ellipsis ix
emotive language 9, 42, 56, 64
exclamation marks viii
exclamations 14
explicit information 4

F

figurative language 12, 42
first person 8
flashbacks 19
flashforwards 19
foreshadowing 19, 31
form 38, 61
formal register 54
fronted adverbials viii
full stops viii
future tense 8

G

generalisations 55
genre 2

H

humour 56
hyperbole 55

I

imperative verbs 14, 42
impersonal tone 54
implicit information 7, 50
informal language x
informal register 54
intensifiers 39
inversion 39
inverted commas vi, ix
irony 56
irregular verbs 8

J

jargon 41
juxtaposition 21

L

letters 63
linear structure 19
line numbers 2
list of three 56, 64
literary fiction 2
local newspapers 62

M

magazines 62
mark schemes 73–78
metaphors 12
motif 12

N

narrative hook 20
narrative viewpoint 20
narrator 20
  first-person narrator 20
  limited narrator 20
  omniscient narrator 20
  second-person narrator 20
  third-person narrator 20
non-chronological structure 19
non-linear structure 19
non-Standard English x
nouns 8

O

object 15
objective writing 42, 55
omission 55
online articles 62
onomatopoeia 11
open letter 63
opinion pieces 62

P

pace 64
paragraphs vii, xi
parenthesis 56
passive voice 15, 54
past tense 8
PEEDL vi, vii
personification 12
perspective 20
planning 30
plot 30
plot twist 31
present tense 8
pronouns xi, 8
proper nouns 8
protagonist 3
punctuation viii
purpose 2, 38, 42, 61
   advise 42
   argue 42
   entertain 42
   explain 42
   inform 42
   instruct 42
   persuade 42

Q

question marks viii
questions 14
quote marks vi
quotes 55

R

register 54
repetition 9, 64
rhetorical devices 42, 56
rhetorical questions 14, 56, 64
rhythm 64

S

sarcasm 56
school newspapers 62
second person 8
semantic field 9
semi-colons ix
sensory language 11
sentence length 14
sentences viii
   complex sentences 15
   compound sentences 15
   sentence inversion 15
   simple sentences 15
setting 2, 30
similes 12
slang x, 41
speeches 64
speech marks ix
spelling x
SQI 47
Standard English x, 54
statements 14
stereotypes 55
structure 18, 19, 61
style 54
subject xi, 15
superlative adjectives 39, 41
symbolism 12

T

tenses xi
theme 12
third person 8
tone 9, 30, 54
   personal tone 54
triplets 56

U

unemotional language 55

V

verbs 8, 15
vocabulary x

W

words and phrases 8

NOTES, DOODLES AND EXAM DATES

....
....
....
....
....
....
....
....
....
....
....
....
....
....

Doodles

Exam dates

Paper 1:

....

Paper 2:

....

ACKNOWLEDGEMENTS

The questions in the ClearRevise textbook are the sole responsibility of the authors and have neither been provided nor approved by the examination board.

Every effort has been made to trace and acknowledge ownership of copyright. The publishers will be happy to make any future amendments with copyright owners that it has not been possible to contact. The publisher would like to thank the following companies and individuals who granted permission for the use of their images in this textbook.

All graphics and images © Shutterstock.

Text on page 5 — Extract from *The Secret Garden* by Frances Hodgson Burnett.

Text on page 6 — Extract from *The Wonderful Wizard of Oz* by L Frank Baum.

Text on page 6 — Extract from *The Thirty-Nine Steps* by John Buchan.

Text on page 6 — Extract from *White Fang* by Jack London.

Text on page 10 — Extract from *The Wonderful Wizard of Oz* by L Frank Baum.

Text on page 13 — Extract from *Call of the Wild* by Jack London.

Text on page 16 — Extract from *Peter Pan* by J M Barrie, reproduced with kind permission from Great Ormond Street Hospital.

Text on page 17 — Extract from *Anne of Green Gables* by L M Montgomery.

Text on page 17 — Extract from *Wind in the Willows* by Kenneth Grahame.

Text on page 22 — Extract from *La Dernière Mobilisation* by W A Dwiggins.

Text on page 24 — Extract from *The Interval* by Vincent O'Sullivan.

Text on page 27 — Extract from *The Literary Sense* by E Nesbit.

Text on page 28 — Extract from *Lonely Places* by Francis Buzzell.

Text on page 39 — Extract from *The Letters of Queen Victoria*.

Text on page 44 — Extract from *Letters of a Woman Homesteader* by Elinore Pruitt Stewart.

Text on page 45 — Extract from *Six Months in Mexico* by Nellie Bly.

Text on page 47 — Extract from *Science in the Kitchen* by E E Kellogg.

Text on page 48 — Extract from *Apes and Monkeys* by R L Garner.

Text on page 49 — Extract from *Notes on Old Edinburgh* by Isabella L Bird.

Text on page 51 — Extract from *A Woman Who Went To Alaska* by Mary Kellogg Sullivan.

Text on page 52 — Extract from *Oxford Mountaineering Essays* by Michael T H Sadler.

Text on page 57 — Extract from *How Girls Can Help Their Country* by Juliette Low.

Text on page 58 — Extract from *The Englishwoman in America* by Isabella L Bird.

EXAMINATION TIPS

With your examination practice, use a boundary approximation using the following table. These boundaries have been calculated as an average across both papers. Be aware that the grade boundaries can vary quite a lot from year to year, so they should be used as a guide only.

Grade	9	8	7	6	5	4	3	2	1
Boundary	79%	73%	67%	60%	53%	46%	34%	21%	9%

1.   Ahead of the exam, one of the best ways to prepare is to read plenty of literary fiction and non-fiction so you're familiar with different writers' methods and perspectives.

2.   Read the questions carefully. Make sure you draw your answers from the section specified in the question. Sometimes it will only be a few lines, other times it might be the whole source.

3.   Make sure you use your time sensibly in the exam. Have a plan for how long you intend to spend on each question, and try to stick to it as closely as you can.

4.   Planning can be helpful for the longer answers, but make sure you don't spend so long writing a plan that you haven't left yourself enough time to write your answer.

5.   Don't panic if a text doesn't include many language techniques (i.e. alliteration, similes, personification). You can still get good marks by analysing the effects of specific words.

6.   Examiners tend to award more marks to answers that focus on a smaller number of details in more depth, than a wider variety of points in limited detail. So don't feel pressured to comment on every little detail you spot, in fact, concentrating on a few key points can often be more worthwhile.

7.   For the creative writing question on Paper 1, avoid using plots from films, computer games and other stories. Often the examiner will recognise that the ideas have been copied from somewhere else, and you will lose marks for creativity.

8.   For the creative writing tasks on both Paper 1 and 2, you need to show a good range of punctuation and vocabulary, however, don't go overboard. Cramming in lots of long words or excessive numbers of semi-colons should be avoided.

9.   For the final question on both papers, focus on quality over quantity. It's almost always better to write a shorter answer which is well structured and has fewer errors, than a long rambling text with lots of mistakes.

10. Both papers award 16 marks for spelling, punctuation and grammar. It's well worth spending 5–10 minutes at the end of the exam editing and checking over your work to make sure you don't throw easy marks away.

Good luck!

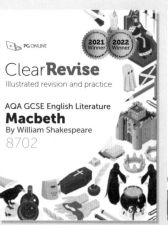

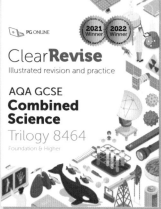
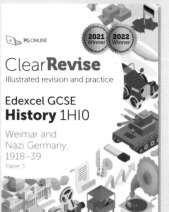
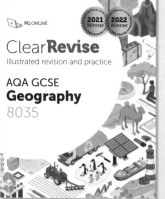